INDIANS OF THE PLAINS

ILLUSTRATED WITH PAINTINGS, PRINTS, DRAWINGS
AND PHOTOGRAPHS OF THE PERIOD

INDIANS

OF THE PLAINS

by the editors of AMERICAN HERITAGE

The Magazine of History

narrative by EUGENE RACHLIS

in consultation with JOHN C. EWERS

Assistant Director
Museum of History and Technology
Smithsonian Institution
Washington, D.C.

Published by

AMERICAN HERITAGE PUBLISHING CO., INC.

Book Trade and Institutional Distribution by

HARPER & ROW

FOREWORD

No OTHER PRIMITIVE people have stirred the interest and imagination of the civilized world as have the North American Indians of the Great Plains. For thousands of years before the first European explorers appeared on the grasslands between the Mississippi River and the Rocky Mountains, the Indians of this region boldly hunted the big, shaggy buffalo on foot. Acquisition of the European horse transformed these plodding footmen into some of the most daring and skillful horsemen in the world. They became more efficient big game hunters, more aggressive and fearsome warriors.

As American settlements moved westward during the nineteenth century the Plains Indians came to know the trader and the trapper, the missionary, the overland trail emigrant, the gold seeker, the cattleman, and the prairie farmer. And as the white man's civilization relentlessly closed in upon them, some of the most powerful tribes fought back valiantly to preserve their traditional hunting grounds. Indian chiefs, experienced only in intertribal warfare, matched wits and courage with experts in military science of the United States Army. The Indian Wars of the Plains provided some of the bitterest battles and some of the most dramatic action in the history of warfare.

Here, in one volume, a history of the Plains Indians and their relations with white men is combined with an account of the traditional customs of these active, picturesque folk. Their methods of hunting, their camp life, warfare and religious ceremonies are interestingly described. The editors of American Heritage have taken pains to assure the authenticity of text and pictures. Illustrations have been selected from original paintings, contemporary photographs, and sketches in the collections of museums and libraries. They include reproductions of works by George Catlin, Carl Bodmer, Paul Kane and other talented artists who visited the West during the years when the Indians and the buffalo still freely roamed the Plains.

This account, telling as it does of those years in which the Plains Indians were literally riding high, helps re-create an era which will always be considered one of the most colorful and exciting in our rich and varied past.

JOHN C. EWERS

SEVENTH PRINTING

LIBRARY OF CONGRESS CATALOG CARD NUMBER: 60–6402

©1960 by American Heritage Publishing Co., Inc., 551 Fifth Avenue, New York, New York, 10017. All rights reserved under Berne and Pan-American Copyright Conventions. Trademark AMERICAN HERITAGE JUNIOR LIBRARY registered United States Patent Office.

This engraving from the cylinder of the famous Colt Repeating Pistol shows Indians fleeing under fire from United States Cavalry.

CONTENTS

THE TRACKLESS LAND

In awe and fear, the army of Francisco Vásquez de Coronado moved slowly across the flat, dry land. Ahead, the earth seemed to stretch to the sky itself. Behind, some of the men grimly noted, the grass over which they traveled did not lie flat, but sprang instantly erect, as if no one had ever passed over it.

There was no trail ahead, and none behind—nothing but a seemingly eternal emptiness on all sides.

The flatness, with the horizon visible in every direction, was overpowering. It was like living in a bowl, one of Coronado's men said, or "as if a man should imagine himself in a three-pint measure, and could see the sky at the edge of it, about a crossbow shot from him." And that sky could be treacherous, too, the men learned, as they marched in searing sun and gritty wind. Sometimes pelting hail dented their heavy

More than fifty million American bison used to roam the western Plains, moving along trails, back and forth between rivers and grazing grounds.

Spanish armor. Only the Indians and the buffalo they passed seemed at home in this strange world.

These were the Great Plains in 1541, the year they were crossed by the Spanish explorer, Coronado, and his men. They were the first Europeans to see that limitless land and the Indians who lived upon it.

Coronado's army was a strange collection of men and animals, and it must have seemed a frightening vision to the Indians. There were more than 200 men on horseback: and horses were so totally new to the Indians that they thought rider and horse were a single animal. The mounted Spaniards in full fighting gear—in mail or in gilded armor which threw back the sun's rays, wearing visored iron helmets and carrying long lances—terrified the nearly naked Indians they met along their route.

Coronado's men crossed the Plains, seeking Quivira, the legendary city of gold.

As if the cavalry were not enough, there were also about 60 armed men afoot, 1000 Mexican Indians, 300 extra horses, 500 head of cattle, 5,000 sheep, and 600 pack mules.

Not even dreams could have prepared the Indians for such a procession. The Plains Indians who first saw and were frightened by Coronado's horsemen were wanderers. The only other humans in their experience would have been other Indians—nomads like themselves, or farmers. Coronado's men said the Indians he met "lived like Arabs."

The Indians were Querechos and Teyas, probably the ancestors of the Plains Apaches. They wandered on foot, following the huge buffalo herds which could keep whole tribes in food and clothing for months. In the winter they traveled to the pueblo villages of what is now New Mexico or to the grass-thatched villages of present day Kansas to trade buffalo robes for corn.

The Querechos and Teyas were large, well-built people. They painted their faces and bodies, and used buffalo skins for clothing and footwear. They lived in skin tents, similar to the tepees which came later, although much smaller. They were skilled in sign language. They practiced a religion which was a form of sun worship.

Coronado found Quivira—but it was not golden. It must have looked much like this village of the Wichita Indians.

Their few belongings were packed on a dog's back or hauled by a dog on a primitive carrier, now called the travois. This is a French word for a device which consisted of two poles and crossbars formed in the shape of the letter A.

The pointed end was tied around the dog's back while the legs of the travois were allowed to drag behind. Goods—buffalo meat, tepee skins and poles, extra clothes—were lashed to the crossbars which were made of wood or rawhide. In this manner, Plains Indian dogs could haul forty or more pounds of gear as far as five or six miles a day.

The Indians, traveling on foot, found all too often that the vast herds of buffalo remained out of reach. And despite their hunters' skill with bow and arrow and lance, there was not enough meat to eat for most of the year.

Coronado's expedition had not been sent out to make history. He and his men had come only for gold and jewels. Somewhere in this land were treasures so vast, they had heard, that there would be enough

Before the Spanish came to America, the Indians had no horses. They could hunt buffalo only on foot. Here braves, disguised in wolfskins, move into arrow-range.

The buffalo was as strange to the Spanish as the horse was to the Indians. Europeans had their first sight of the huge monster in this drawing, made in 1554.

for each soldier to spend his days as a grandee, without ever marching again under such a bitter sky.

There had been one terrible disappointment already. The Seven Cities of Cibola, which were supposed to hold fabulous wealth, had turned out to be poor Indian pueblos made of clay. There were no rich harvests; no gold, nor silver nor silks. Instead of gold there had been intense fighting. Some Spanish dead had been left behind among the Indian dead, and of those marching on, many carried battle wounds.

Now they were heading for still a new goal, a city called Quivira. It had been described to them in such wondrous, yet such exact terms, that none doubted its existence or its gold. In Quivira, they had been told, the trees were hung with tinkling golden bells, and pitchers and bowls and dishes were made of solid silver and gold. The man who told them of Quivira, an Indian called El Turco ("the Turk"—because his headdress resembled a turban) was acting as their guide. With the Turk walking beside Coronado, at the head of the army, Quivira would soon be found. Somewhere short of the distant horizon they would reach that city, and its golden treasures would reward them for their hardships.

But there was to be no reward. The Great Plains were too much for these early intruders. Soldiers hunting for buffalo left no trail on the ground. The men could not find their way back to camp. Horses wandered off across the prairie and were never seen again.

When it became clear to Coronado that his army could move no faster than its slowest animals, he had to split his forces. Most of the soldiers, Indians, and animals were ordered to turn back. Coronado proceeded to Quivira with a handful of cavalry and infantrymen, living off the buffalo they found.

This smaller party was able to move faster, and at last, it came to Quivira. There they found nothing but a group of Indian villages somewhere near what is now Dodge City, Kansas. The houses were thatched with grass. The Indians were farmers tilling the soil for squash, beans, and corn.

The Spanish could see at once that this was not the golden Quivira described by the Turk. The nearest thing to gold they saw was a copper medallion worn by a chief. The Turk had invented the whole story as part of an Indian plan to lead Coronado and his men to their deaths on the Plains. For this

treachery, the Turk was killed by Coronado's officers.

In the spring of 1542, Coronado and his men retreated from the Great Plains, back to Mexico where the expedition had started. There was no gold at Cibola or Quivira, or anywhere else on the Plains. There was nothing but wasteland, fit only for Indians and buffalo.

Coronado's men headed south and the grass behind them rose back in place, leaving no trace that these invaders had ever passed that way.

This Wichita chief and his tribesmen were the probable descendants of the Indians Coronado found in Quivira.

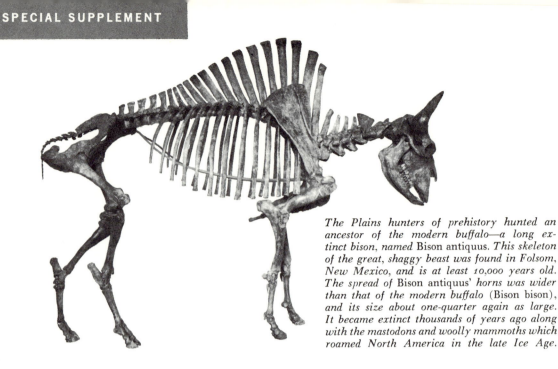

The Plains hunters of prehistory hunted an ancestor of the modern buffalo—a long extinct bison, named Bison antiquus. This skeleton of the great, shaggy beast was found in Folsom, New Mexico, and is at least 10,000 years old. The spread of Bison antiquus' horns was wider than that of the modern buffalo (Bison bison), and its size about one-quarter again as large. It became extinct thousands of years ago along with the mastodons and woolly mammoths which roamed North America in the late Ice Age.

The Indians of prehistory used neither horses nor bows and arrows in hunting Bison antiquus. Instead they might wait at a water hole, as shown here, and plunge their stone-tipped spears into the monster's sides. Stone spearheads, like those shown at right, have been found fixed in the spines of bison.

An archaeologist examines the remains of an earth lodge in an Arikara village, near the mouth of the Cheyenne River in South Dakota. Occupied between 1750–90, it contained a storage bin, at right, used to store grain.

INDIANS OF PREHISTORY

Perhaps 20,000 years ago the first Indians began coming to North America from Siberia, by way of Alaska. From them, and from those who followed, descended all the varied tribes of North and South America.

When Columbus landed, in 1492, there were about 900,000 Indians living in what is now Canada and the United States. None of the Indians of North America used the wheel, or kept any domestic animal except the dog. They had no alphabet, and no knowledge of the use of iron. Their implements and weapons were made of bone, chipped stone, shell, and copper.

Archaeologists have found remains of villages in the river valleys of the Plains, where Indians lived and tended their farms. But thousands of years before the first farmers appeared in the area, Plains Indians lived as nomads, or in caves. They hunted the ground sloth, the bison and the early wild horses and camels which roamed the broad prairies in the late Ice Age.

Both the wild horse and the camel became extinct long before the time of Columbus. But the bison's descendants prospered so well that by the time of Coronado there were probably more than 50,000,000 buffalo on the Plains.

This 650-year-old clay pot, found near the above village, was made without the aid of a potter's wheel.

These three stone spearheads, along with sixteen others, were found under the floor of a cave in the Sandia Mountains of New Mexico. Ranging between two and four inches long, they had been painstakingly chipped and flaked from pieces of quartz and obsidian. They belong to the late Ice Age, and may be from 12,000 to 20,000 years old.

Prong-horned Antelopes

THE GREAT PLAINS

The 98th meridian—an invisible line running from the North Pole to the South Pole—cuts across the United States from Valley City, North Dakota to San Marcos, Texas. It is sometimes called the "disaster line," for west of it, and reaching to the foothills of the Rocky Mountains, lies a vast land whose average annual rainfall is only twenty inches, and whose wide extremes of

Prairie Wolves, or Coyotes

Prairie Dogs

J. J. Audubon, famous for his illustrations of birds, also sketched the animal life of North America. These pictures of his show some of the animals most often seen on the Plains.

Even after a prairie blizzard, the buffalo was not safe from hunters on snowshoes; for, as the artist has shown, the beasts could be killed easily, as they floundered in the drifts. Details are incorrect, however, as Indians never wore war bonnets on a hunt, nor summer clothes in the freezing cold.

Late in the hot prairie summer, as the crops ripened, Indian women built shelters in the fields. There they stayed until harvest, frightening crows from the corn.

temperature have brought havoc to men, crops, and animals.

No other area in the country is buffeted by such unpredictable weather—blizzards, hailstorms, tornadoes, drought, searing heat, or that warm, dry wind called the chinook.

It is an area of grassland. Only near rivers and streams—or in an isolated area such as the Black Hills—does one see trees. Mesquite, thorn bushes, and sagebrush are common. Few wild plants, such as the prairie turnip and the chokecherry, are edible. Rivers run through the Plains, but few are navigable, and sometimes during dry spells they disappear altogether.

"The World and the Two Gods of the Weather," a Plains Indian drawing, pictures the struggle between summer and winter. Inside the circle, which is the world, stand the North God, Wa-ze-at-tah, in a snowstorm; and the South God, Eto-kah, in a rainstorm. The North God has a pack of wolves as his allies; the South God, a crow and a plover. Each spring and fall, the gods will do battle, ". . . for as long as the world shall stand."

RED MEN ON HORSEBACK

In the summer of 1834, George Catlin wrote: "A Comanche on his feet is out of his element, and comparatively almost as awkward as a monkey on the ground, without a limb or a branch to cling to; but the moment he lays his hand upon his horse, his face even becomes handsome, and he gracefully flies away like a different being."

The Comanche were one of the most important tribes which resided on the Southern Plains. Catlin, a lawyer turned painter, was one of the first Americans to live among the Plains Indians.

Catlin was deeply impressed with the horsemanship of the Indians. Yet, amazingly enough, at the time he saw them, in the summer of 1834,

"Catching the Wild Horse" is one of many paintings of western Indians by George Catlin, the famous American artist who first visited the Plains tribes in 1832.

horses had been an important part of Plains Indian life for no more than 100 years. Some of the tribes—especially in the north—had owned horses for even less time than that.

No one knows for certain how the Plains Indians obtained their first horses. Of Coronado's 554 horses, only two were mares, so that even if a number were lost during the search for Quivira, it is unlikely that they were the original source.

Most students of early Indian history now believe that the Plains tribes got their first horses from the early Spanish settlements in what are now New Mexico and Arizona. Many of these missions and ranches hired Indians to take care of their animals. In this way members of the southern tribes learned early to ride and handle horses.

The Spaniards may have foreseen what horses could do for these primitive people, for they tried to prevent them from getting any. But despite Spanish watchfulness, Indians managed to steal large numbers. In 1680, an Indian revolt in the Southwest so terrified the Spanish that they left the territory, and hundreds of horses stampeded into the open country. With miles of grazing land available, the herds roamed freely for years. These escaped horses grew wild in their ways, increased, and became a lasting source of supply for the Indians.

Slowly, through the passing years, horses moved north on the Plains—as the Indians stole them, traded for them, or captured them on the open range. At first, some tribes called them "mystery dogs" or "elk dogs," and occasionally ate them. Soon they learned that the horse was superior to the dog as a means of transportation.

A horse travois was devised which could carry loads of up to 200 pounds—four times more than could be packed on a dog travois. And horses could carry these loads twice as far each day as the dog carried the lighter load.

Eventually, the Indians learned to ride these wonderful animals; probably the southern tribes—having seen the Spaniards—rode first. Later, the Northern Plains Indians

got on horseback. One by one, as the tribes mastered and developed the art of riding, their lives changed until a new kind of Indian roamed the Plains.

Village tribes dropped their crude farm tools and took to hunting buffalo. Out of the woods and plains of northeastern Minnesota came the Cheyenne, and their allies for generations, the Arapaho. From the foothills of the Rocky Mountains came the Comanche, an offshoot of the Shoshoni, both of whom were sometimes called the Snake Indians.

From the banks of the Mississippi in Minnesota and Wisconsin came the Dakota tribes, better known as the Sioux. The Crow, great enemies of the Cheyenne, Arapaho, and Dakota, moved westward from the banks of the Missouri. And some—like the Kiowa Apache—came from places that even tribal legend and story could no longer recall.

The Blackfoot, to the north, first saw the horse around 1730 when their deadly enemies, the Shoshoni, made a mounted attack on a group of them. The result was disaster to the Blackfoot band. They learned at once, as did the other tribes, that from that time on, no unmounted Indian could ever again stand against enemies on horseback.

The horse made nomadic life more attractive than ever before. With horses, tribes could travel 500 to 800 miles in the spring, summer, and fall, and keep pace with the

THE PLAINS TRIBES—1830

SARSI

PLAINS CREE

BLACKFOOT

GROS VENTRES

ASSINIBOIN

N.D. MINN.

+HIDATSA
+MANDAN

EASTERN SIOUX

CROW

+ARIKARA

S.D.

Missouri R.

Yellowstone R.

NEZ PERCÉS

MONT.

SH.

IDAHO

WYO.

WESTERN SIOUX

Minnesota R.

Missouri R.

IOWA

+IOWA

SHOSHONE

North Platte R.

NEBR.

+PONCA

+OMAHA

V.

UTAH

ARAPAHO

COLO.

+PAWNEE

Platte R.

+OTO and MISSOURI

MO.

UTE

AND CHEYENNE

South Platte R.

KANS.

+KANSA

Colorado R.

ARIZ.

N. M.

KIOWA and KIOWA APACHE

OKLA.

+OSAGE

Arkansas R.

ARK.

+WICHITA

Red R.

COMANCHE

Rio Grande

TEXAS

+ denotes semi-sedentary tribes

buffalo migrations. Hunting on horseback meant the difference between feast and famine.

Warfare became an even greater game. Stealing—or capturing—horses from other tribes, and later from the white men, was considered the proper and necessary thing for a man to do at any time. A skillful horse thief, according to an American army officer, could "crawl into a bivouac where a dozen men were sleeping, each with his horse tied to his wrist by a lariat, cut a rope within six feet of a sleeper's person, and get off with the horse without waking a soul."

Horses were wealth, and a man's importance was measured by the number of horses he owned. In ceremonies which called for generous gifts, horses ranked highest. At the birth of a son, some Indians would give away a pony.

Men paid for desirable things with horses. A brave who wanted to marry a pretty girl might pay her family up to ten horses for the privilege. Indians often bartered horses for guns and ammunition. Children were taught to ride and to care for colts; as they grew older they were given larger, swifter horses. And when a warrior died,

Alfred Jacob Miller's painting, "Snake and Sioux Indians on the Warpath," shows how warriors used their horses as shields against enemy spears and arrows.

his horse was buried with him so that they could ride together through eternity.

In the years from roughly 1750 to 1800 (during which time all but a few village tribes had acquired large herds of horses) the Plains Indians captured wild horses, tamed them and trained them to perfection for buffalo hunting and warfare. Often, at hunts or in battle the Indians rode bareback. Later they added a simple saddle made of buffalo skin, and used buffalo thongs (rawhide) as bridles.

Catlin was continually amazed by what the Comanches could do. He thought them "the most extraordinary horsemen that I have seen yet in all my travels." An Indian was able, he said, "to drop his body upon the side of his horse, effectively screened from his enemies' weapons as he [lies] in a horizontal position behind the body of his horse, with his heel hanging over the horse's back; by which he has the power of throwing himself up again, and changing to the other side of the horse if necessary.

"In this wonderful condition, he will hang whilst his horse is at the fullest speed, carrying with him his bow and his shield, and also his long lance of fourteen feet in length, all or either of which he will wield upon his enemy as he passes; rising and throwing his arrows over the horse's back, or with ease and equal success under the horse's neck."

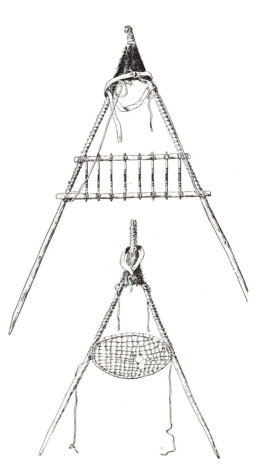

Before horses came to the Plains, Indians had no animals but dogs to carry heavy burdens. These dog travois were used by Blackfoot (top) and Cree (bottom).

To many whites the horse and the Indian often seemed blurred into one figure—a single animal like the mythological centaur. The horse brought the Plains Indians freedom, pleasure, and wealth and made possible that golden age of their existence, which ran from about 1800 until after the Civil War. The Plains Indians of those years were indeed, no less than what Walter Prescott Webb, one of the most brilliant historians of the Plains, called them, "the red knights of the prairie."

INDIAN CATTLE

Of all the things the horse put within reach of the Plains Indians, none was as important as the buffalo. The big, ugly, shaggy animal represented life itself. He provided all that was needed for food, clothing, and shelter. His migrations decided where and how the Indians were to live.

Instead of Plains Indians, Americans might better have called them the Buffalo Indians. Their time of glory was simply the time when they hunted buffalo. When the buffalo disappeared, the roving life of the Plains Indians also disappeared.

In the days of plenty, it was hard to believe that a time would come when there would not be enough buffalo. As long ago as Coronado's first appearance, men had wondered at the size of the herds. Coronado wrote the King of Spain that he saw so many "it is imposible to number them, for while I was journeying through these plains . . . there was not a day that I lost sight of them."

Three hundred years later he was echoed by Captain Benjamin Bonneville, an American soldier: "As far as the eye could see the country seemed absolutely blacked by innumerable herds." Eye-witness accounts told how it took one herd of buffalo three days to swim the Missouri; how herds of two million, three million, even four million buffalo covered the earth. Sometimes, the mass of animals was ten miles long and eight miles wide.

The Indians were no less impressed than the white men by the size of the herds. There always had been buffalo: there always would be

In this hunt, galloping riders surround a large herd of buffalo. Strays are being driven over the cliff and killed.

buffalo. The Plains Indians could ask no more. Some tribes even spoke of the buffalo as their cattle.

Even as a child the Indian knew the importance of buffalo. Before they had teeth, children sucked bits of buffalo meat. As they grew older, they learned to know that the meat from the cow made better eating than that from the bull. Buffalo tongue was a special treat, and served as a sacred food in many ceremonies. Great feasts followed successful hunts. Large pieces of the newly-killed buffalo were roasted over an open fire, and handed out to feed all who were hungry.

It was not surprising that the In-

In winter, Indians on snowshoes could overtake buffalo bogged down in deep snow.

dians held tribal celebrations when they feasted on fresh buffalo meat. For, during most of the year, the Plains Indians ate preserved meat, which had been saved for use during the long periods when fresh meat was impossible to find. The most popular form of preserving buffalo meat was as pemmican. This was made by pounding the sun-dried meat with a stone hammer until it became a pulp. The pulp was then mixed with buffalo fat and stored in bags made of buffalo skin. Meat was also preserved by drying long, thin strips in the sun. These were then packed with alternate layers of uncooked buffalo fat and berries. It was kept in a buffalo skin packet (called a parfleche) which looked like a giant envelope. Food was only one of the many things the buffalo contributed to the Plains Indians. Buffalo skin was used in innumerable ways. The hides of the buffalo killed in winter were covered with heavy fur. From these winter hides the Indians made mittens, caps, moccasins, and robes, which could be used as blankets or as a kind of overcoat. The animals killed in the spring and fall did not have heavy fur. Their skins were

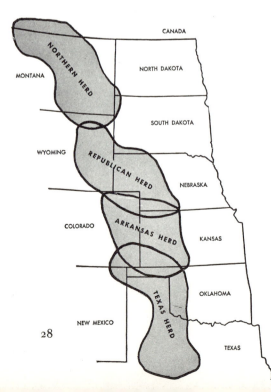

Buffalo herds hunted by the Plains Indians stretched from Texas into Canada.

28

used as shirts, leggings, and dresses, when skins of deer, elk, and mountain sheep were not available. The even thinner skins of buffalo calves were used as underclothes.

The buffalo skin was tough and waterproof and, with care, lasted for years. The bull's hide was tougher than the hide of the cow. This made it useful for almost all the gear needed for the horse, and especially for attaching the travois.

Wet thongs of rawhide were used to tie the heads of hammers and clubs to handles. When the rawhide dried it shrank and held the head firmly in place. The thick skin from around the buffalo bull's neck made an excellent shield when dried and hardened. Summer skins of the cows were used for making tepees.

But the Indians had use for more than the skin. The bones of the buffalo were used as tools for farming; the sinews were used as thread and, when twisted, made excellent bowstrings; the horns were used as spoons, ladles, and cups; the stomach was cleaned and made into a bag for carrying food or water; sometimes it served as a cooking pot. The dung of the buffalo—called "buffalo chips"—was used as fuel.

When the Plains Indians discovered that the white men valued buffalo hides, they set up a trading operation. And thus the buffalo was able to provide them with some of the things the white men offered— kettles for cooking; iron for arrow heads; guns and ammunition.

And so the buffalo hunt took on vast importance for the Plains tribes. Around it were developed many of

Many Plains Indians trapped buffalo in a pound, or corral of logs. Here a herd is being driven between two lines of shouting, waving tribesmen.

Once inside the corral, the animals were easily killed with bows and arrows.

the Indian rituals, in which entire tribes would join, to pray for a world in which there would always be buffalo.

When the cold winter had passed, when the pemmican was all but used up, the Indians knew that the annual migration of the herds would start again. Small hunting bands which had spent the winter in separate shelters came together as a tribe. Tepees were set up, and in the days which followed, as scouts scattered to find the buffalo herd, there would be games and songs.

When the herd was sighted, a camp was selected, and the entire group moved to it in an orderly fashion. There was great excitement on the day of the hunt, as the men put their gear in order and the women and girls prepared for their chores—the skinning, cooking, and stripping of the meat for drying.

Before the Plains Indians became horsemen, the buffalo hunt took various forms, all of them based on the fact that the buffalo is not a very intelligent animal and has poor eyesight. One method was called "the surround" and consisted simply of many hunters forming a circle around part of a herd, and forcing the animals to move about in helter-

skelter fashion. The bewildered animals then became easy targets for a good shot with a bow and arrow.

Sometimes the buffalo herd was stampeded over the edge of a cliff. They were driven by men shouting and waving robes from behind a line of stones leading to the cliff. The animals would either fall to their deaths, or be so crippled that they could be easily killed.

Another form of buffalo hunt was called impounding. This method was preferred by the Cree and Assiniboin, although the Blackfoot and Crow also used it.

First, a corral had to be built. Leading to the opening were fences which narrowed in toward the corral in the shape of a large V. After scouts found the buffalo herd, it was

Crow buffalo-hide shield; Sioux pipe bag and painted buffalo-hide parfleche. (Bottom row) Crow, Sioux, and Cree moccasins, with quillwork (left) and beads; Sioux buffalo-horn spoon; Cree tom-tom; and small Blackfoot pouch with quill design.

These fleshers and scrapers—bone and iron tools— were used by Indian women for dressing buffalo hides.

Plains Indian to show his valor while hunting. Astride a well-trained horse, the Indian could rush close to an animal, shoot it with a bow and arrow, and then continue on to the next and the next, until the racing herd thundered beyond his reach. Afterwards it was easy to tell which hunter had killed a particular buffalo. Each Indian's arrows could be identified by the way he tied the arrowhead to the shaft or by the color of the feathers. Some courageous hunters preferred to use a short lance with an iron head; killing a buffalo with this weapon while riding a fast-moving horse took even more skill than using a bow and arrow.

Buffalo hunting depended, of course, on the skill of a man's horse. A well-trained hunting horse—fast,

lured toward the corral, sometimes by an Indian who covered his body with a calf skin and imitated the bleating of a young buffalo; sometimes fire was used. Once the herd started on its way, other members of the tribe would move in from behind to keep the buffalo headed in the right direction.

Despite these methods, the Plains Indian did not fully gain the upper hand until he began hunting buffalo on horseback. With the horse, far greater numbers of buffalo could be killed on one hunt.

The horse also permitted the

When a migrating herd had to cross a river, it often fell prey to attack. Here Indians swim out into the Missouri River to kill the slowly swimming beasts.

After the buffalo was killed, women skinned the woolly hide from the carcass and butchered choice portions of the meat.

alert, intelligent—was worth two or three pack horses. But even the best horse might be knocked over by a charging buffalo, or might trip in a hole and throw his rider into the mass of stampeding buffalo. The hunt was a dangerous business, but that only made it more enjoyable to the Plains Indians.

No matter which hunting method was used, there were strict rules for a large tribal hunt. No man could start hunting on his own, or even disturb the herds. The penalties were heavy for those who broke the rules: their weapons were destroyed, their clothing torn, and they were disgraced before the entire group. Young men of proven bravery in battle acted as policemen during a hunt and made sure that the chief's instructions were carried out.

Despite the seriousness with which the rules were taken, a buffalo hunt was a happy and exciting event. Little boys on their colts followed the older hunters, to shoot the straggling buffalo calves. The poor and the old never went hungry. There was always someone generous enough to share his catch with those who had neither the horses nor the strength to capture buffalo for themselves.

When the hunt was over, the women moved in with sharp knives and pack horses. Swiftly they cut up the animals, and loaded them on horses. In the summer, when there were plenty of buffalo, only the best parts of the meat were kept. In the fall or winter, nearly every edible part of the animal was saved. Not counting the bones, this would amount to about five hundred pounds of freshly butchered meat—a much greater load than any single horse could carry.

But the results of a buffalo hunt were reckoned in more than meat and bones and hides. All winter long the Indians had fed on pemmican, occasionally shooting small game or a winter buffalo, but mainly trying to stay alive until the warm days came again. But with the hunt came a time of games, feasting and singing, dancing and storytelling, of tracking down the vast buffalo herds, of making plans for battle with traditional enemies—a time of renewal for the entire tribe.

THE LIFE OF THE WANDERER

The life of the Plains Indians was a life of movement and change. The fact that they were nomads influenced their food, housing, and clothing; their government, warfare, customs, rituals, and religion.

Except for the winter encampment, when single families or small bands of families settled down as well as they could to protect themselves against the cold, snow, and wind, the Plains tribes were con-

When the Sioux moved camp, a group of braves scouted ahead, alert for enemies. Women and children tended the horses and dogs which were harnessed to the travois.

stantly in motion. Some of the tribes on the High Plains—Dakota, Cheyenne, Comanche, Blackfoot—ranged vast distances on land which was vaguely identified as their own. But they never had a fixed residence, or headquarters. Other tribes—Hidatsa, Mandan, Pawnee, Omaha—had built more permanent villages in the river valleys of the eastern Plains. There they raised corn and squash, as their ancestors had done.

Tribes which followed migrating buffalo lived in tepees, like these of the Sioux.

But they, too, became wanderers when they had to leave their villages, in summer, to seek the huge, migrating herds of buffalo.

After they began to use horses, the Plains Indians grew even more nomadic, and no longer led the lives of their ancestors. They had to learn new ways of fighting, and of housing and clothing themselves. To answer their needs, they devised the horse travois, the short bow, and a larger portable shelter, made of buffalo skins. Today, few signs of Plains Indian culture are better known than the buffalo-skin tepee. The word itself comes from the Dakota, but we use it now to identify every tribe's portable home.

The buffalo-skin tepee gave excellent protection against the changeable weather of the Plains. It was a simple structure to build, to carry, to put up, and to take down. Tribes built their tepees in various styles, but the general pattern was the same. The size of a tepee was determined by the wealth of its owner and the number of people who lived in it. Around a basic support of three or four poles, which varied in length depending on the size of the tepee, as many as ten or twelve more would be placed.

Tepees were simply furnished; nomadic tribes could not burden themselves or their horses with too many belongings. Beds were usually made of buffalo robes laid on the ground. But among the Arapaho, beds were raised from the ground and had back rests. There were no tables and chairs, although the Blackfoot and Crow made back rests from willow sticks and sinew.

Directly in the center of the tepee the Indians built their fires for warmth and cooking. Above the fireplace was a vent, a hole purposely left in the tent, with a pair of skin "ears" which could be adjusted to direct the smoke's escape. The entrance to the tepee was covered by a small flap of skin.

Most of the tribes painted the outsides of their tepees. The designs were determined by the dreams of the tepee owner. When a vision came to him he would seek out a skilled painter and have him paint his tepee exactly as he had dreamed it. A popular form of painting was one in which the owner of the tepee and his wife were represented by a pair of buffalo. These often ran around the entire outside of the tepee. Above the animals a band of black with white spots signified the dark night and the stars. Below, a band of red symbolized earth.

Tribes living in fixed villages used tepees only when traveling. Their permanent homes were earth lodges. These varied from tribe to

A warrior holds an enemy scalp, in this first picture to show a tepee interior.

tribe, but essentially they were of similar design: low buildings made of wooden frames covered with earth, bark, or thatched grass. Some circular earth lodges were large enough to house forty people or more, and all their belongings, including dogs and horses. Others were made for single families.

This earth lodge village of the Hidatsa Indians stood on a bluff overlooking the Knife River in central North Dakota.

The Mandan buffalo robe (right) and Cree woman's dress (below) were collected by Lewis and Clark on their famous expedition, and sent to Thomas Jefferson in 1805. The robe is the oldest painted buffalo hide in existence. It pictures an attack of Sioux and Arikara on the Mandan tribe in 1797.

Hudson's Bay traders supplied the blue "pony" beads and brass buttons used on this Indian girl's dress. It is the oldest example of Plains Indian beadwork.

In building an earth lodge, a circular area was first dug to a depth which would allow for people to sit comfortably on the outer edge, with their feet touching the floor. Post and beams were then fitted into place. The Plains Indians did not have nails, nor did they use pegs the way some white people did before the iron nail was invented. Post and beams were either carefully cut to fit at the proper place or they were tied together with rawhide thongs. Some of the lodges had domed or conical roofs, others were flat. Four to eight posts, about ten feet high, were set up at the center. Beams were fitted from them to posts around the outside circumference.

Rafters were then laid across the beams, and covered with branches. Sods of earth, laid on top of the branches, completed the roof. The sides were also covered with sod. The entrance was a passageway six to ten feet long, with an opening covered by a buffalo skin. A hole was left in the center of the roof above the fireplace, sometimes covered with a frame of branches on which skins would be placed.

The interiors of the lodges also followed a fairly well-established pattern. Around the wall were placed stalls for the horses, beds for the people, raised platforms for food, firewood, tools, implements, and weapons. Cooking utensils were kept near the fireplace. In all lodges, one large area was reserved as a sacred place for prayer. The medicine bundle with all its revered objects was also kept here. It was usually set up on poles so that it would never have to touch the ground.

To many Europeans and Americans, the most common picture of the Plains Indians is that of a group of mounted warlike young men, their feathered bonnets streaming behind them. Unfortunately, this picture is not altogether accurate. Although the war bonnet was used by many of the Plains tribes, especially by branches of the Dakota or Sioux, it was usually worn only on special ceremonial occasions. It took courage for leaders to wear them in battle; for their bonnets' trailing feathers marked them out for special attention from the enemy. Most of the year the Plains Indians wore no headdress at all. On cold days, many wore caps with ear flaps.

The Plains Indian paid more attention to his hair than to the hat which covered it. It had a special meaning to the Indian, and like the biblical Samson, he felt that he gained strength and life from his hair. Most Plains Indians allowed it to grow long and fall freely; later men and women started to braid it. Buffalo fat was often used to keep it in place.

The Mandan chief, Four Bears, or Mato-tope, wears a war bonnet decorated with buffalo horns. The hand painted on his shirt shows he has killed a foe in hand-to-hand combat. His sleeves and his leggings are hung with enemy scalp-locks.

Frequently, the manner in which the hair was worn served to identify the wearer's tribe. The Crow Indians favored a high pompadour. The Pawnee shaved their hair, except for a strip from the forehead to the back of the neck. Sometimes, as with the Omaha, a lock of hair was separated and braided and decorated

39

In 1833, the Swiss artist Carl Bodmer traveled up the Missouri River into Montana. There he painted this large camp of Blackfoot Indians.

with feathers. Not all Plains Indians believed in scalping their enemies, but all of them were eager to keep their own hair from falling into enemy hands. Some went so far as to burn the hair they had cut off.

Plains Indian men wore as little as possible, especially while hunting. Their workaday costume often consisted of no more than a breech cloth. Sometimes they wore deerskin tunics, or shirts of calico or flannel received in trade from white men. In cold weather, they covered themselves with buffalo robes. The women wore simple dresses and knee-length leggings made of cloth or deerskin. They never wore their fancy dresses for work around the camp. In warm weather, boys under ten usually wore no clothes at all.

The Indians' ceremonial clothing was highly decorative. Men's shirts and leggings did not tell as much of a story as their headdresses did. But their battle shirts were particularly interesting. Their designs, determined by dreams, were supposed to prevent injury. Some of the designs were simply painted horizontal stripes. Others were elaborately made with quills and beads, or ermine skins which were hung from the neck and sleeves.

Women often decorated their ceremonial clothes with elk's teeth. Crow and Blackfoot women especially prized them. Only two teeth from one animal were ever used for dress decoration. This meant that only the wife of a fine hunter could decorate her dress with any number of them. Some dresses boasted as many as 300 teeth worked into a pattern. Less fortunate women settled for designs using porcupine quills or beads, or with imitation elk teeth made of bone. After trade began with the white man, many an Indian woman's dress was decorated with swatches of red flannel imported from England.

As footwear, the Plains Indians had for generations worn the simple pieces of leather we know as moccasins. They were usually undecorated, but when worn with ceremonial clothes, even moccasins had bright designs. For normal wear, they were made of a single piece of soft leather folded over to fit the foot. In the winter, they were made from the skin of the winter buffalo with the fur turned inward. Later, when the Plains Indians saw the white man's hard-soled shoes, they began to make moccasins with hard rawhide soles on soft skin uppers.

In all things, from the weapons he wore to the tepee over his head, the Plains Indian never forgot that he was a wanderer who traveled by horse to follow the buffalo. Only possessions which fitted that way of life could be kept. Housing which could be quickly struck in one place and quickly erected in another was the only kind he could use. Utensils and clothes which were light, and easy to load on a travois or pack horse were the only kind he could carry. For his was the life of the wanderer—a life full of movement and endless change.

The buffalo robe in Bodmer's drawing is decorated with a stripe of porcupine quills, and painted with battle scenes. Above it is a peace pipe, or calumet.

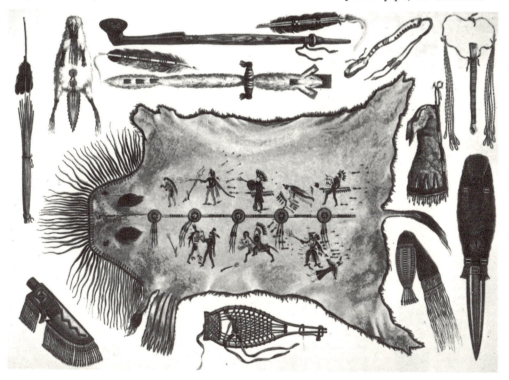

The wealthy men of the tribe were expected to give feasts and presents to the poor, and to visitors. The above picture, by George Catlin, called "A Dog Feast," was painted after Catlin and a party of fur traders were entertained by a band of Sioux in the 1830's.

During the nineteenth century, as Plains Indian tribes were slowly forced to sign treaties with the United States government and move to reservations, the Indian agent became well-known to the red man. Agents worked for the Bureau of Indian Affairs, which had been set up in 1824. Often they lived on reservations, caring for the Indians in their charge. When serious problems arose, delegations of chiefs might go to Washington to meet the Great White Father. In 1870, these chiefs held their peace conference with President U.S. Grant.

Among most Plains Indians, any able man—such as this Mandan leader—might be made a chief.

"Indian Council," by Alfred Jacob Miller, shows a Plains Indian chief holding a pow-wow with the elders of the tribe. Chiefs rarely made decisions without talking with the elders—men who had become important through acts of generosity, through bravery in warfare, or through the experience and wisdom of age.

TRIBAL LAW

In Plains Indian society some families owned more horses than did others, and had larger tepees. But this did not prevent a boy from a poor family from gaining wealth—by stealing horses or winning them in battle—and marrying into a rich family. Wealthy men felt required to be generous to the poor, and to give large feasts and handsome presents.

No Plains Indian chief had supreme authority over his people. Chiefs who were known to be good peacemakers were often sought to arbitrate disputes. But serious questions affecting the group were most often decided in a council of leading men.

"Bear Dance" by George Catlin, illustrates an initiation ceremony of a war society. There were a number of secret societies in each tribe, each with its own animal god. Leaders of the societies—not always the tribal chief— led war parties in battle, policed the great buffalo hunts, and managed tribal assemblies.

Differences within the tribe were usually settled by persuasion. Murder was rare, but when it occurred, the Cheyenne usually exiled the offender from the tribe. The Crow, on the other hand, made the murderer pay goods and horses to the victim's family. Men who acted against the welfare of the tribe might face loss of property, exile, or even death.

Afraid Eagle

Good Weasel

Cloud Shield

Slow Bear

Top Man

Red Cloud

Chief Red Cloud, of the Oglala Teton Sioux, was one of the most famous of all Plains Indian leaders. He counted eighty coups in battle and probably took his name from the horde of scarlet-blanketed warriors who followed him, and "covered the hillside like a red cloud." In 1866-7, he was at war with the United States, but later signed a treaty of peace, and moved to the Pine Ridge Reservation in South Dakota. There, in 1884, he was asked to take a census of his tribe. Signatures of some of his warriors appear above. At left, an Indian asks "How many?" in sign language. Below, Sioux Chief Eagle Bull makes the gesture for "bull," as he starts to signal his name.

SIGN LANGUAGE AND

Among the Plains Indians varieties of dialects of six distinct languages were spoken. Nor were Indian languages simple, as many people believe. Large vocabularies and complicated grammar were often present. Even within the same family grouping of Indians, such as the Sioux, tribes were often unable to communicate except through the sign language.

Sign language was a major invention of the Plains Indians. No one knows how it started, but perhaps it was begun when several tribes of strangers found themselves

Plains Indians had no alphabet, but like the Chinese they used a form of picture writing, in which each sign stood for a word or an idea. At right is a portion of a buffalo-hide calendar or "winter count" as the Indians called it, for the years 1800-1871. It was made by Lone Dog, a Dakota Sioux. Beginning at the center and spiraling outward, each picture tells the chief event of a single year. Events recorded here include an outbreak of smallpox, the first capture of wild horses, and some bloody fights with the Crows and Gros Ventres.

The sign-language gesture for "antelope," placed beside the symbol for "antelope" in picture writing, (left) shows how closely related these two forms of communication could be.

Indians signaled to each other over great distances on the broad Plains by means of smoke, mirrors, or simply by wigwagging with a buffalo robe. Message sent here: "Buffalo discovered!"

PICTURE WRITING

camped nearby on a buffalo hunt. It must have existed in prehistory, since Coronado's men saw Indians making use of it. It became so effective over the years that friendly tribes who lived close to one another for long periods of time never bothered to learn their neighbor's language. Signs did as well.

In sign language, a white man was designated by drawing a finger across the forehead—the sign for "hat." Later, a number of "hat-wearers" learned sign language, and were able to "talk" as freely to Indians as the Indians "talked" among themselves.

In summer, one of the Indians' favorite pastimes was a fast ball game in which a small hair ball was struck with a curved stick made of cherry-wood. Catlin's painting shows young Sioux women at play.

"Indian Horse Race," by Paul Kane, pictures a Blackfoot camp, with two riders streaking past. Races of two to four miles were run, usually at the time of the summer buffalo hunts, when the entire tribe could enjoy them. Indians bet heavily on favorites, so judges were always present to insure fair play.

Indian children played with toys, just as do children everywhere. Indian-made toys, above, include two buffaloes, behind which stand a spotted or pinto Indian pony, a male doll, and an elk or wapiti.

INDIAN SPORTS AND PASTIMES

The Plains Indians enjoyed their leisure. Tribal life offered many occasions for dancing, for storytelling, and for games. Indian children played games of make-believe. Young boys fought mock battles and pretended to hunt buffalo. Young girls built small tepees for their dolls and played house.

But games were not for children alone. Grown men were fond of guessing games—many of which could be used for gambling. In one game, two small bones, identical except for a mark on one, were hidden in both hands. The object was to guess which hand held the unmarked bit of bone. Points were awarded for each correct guess and the person first reaching the proper total was the winner. He usually received something as valuable as a horse.

Women played a kind of dice game using marked plum stones; men played a hoop-and-pole game. Frequently, too, Indian encampments were treated to the excitement of a shooting match, or a horse race.

In winter, when the rivers were frozen, men, women, and children played games on the ice. Here men are playing a ball game something like lacrosse. Children, too, went sliding on the ice on sleds made with buffalo-bone runners.

Indian women playing plum stones.

LIFE OF AN INDIAN BRAVE

From childhood on, an Indian boy dreamed of the day he would ride off to the hunt, or to war, with the men. By the time he was seven or eight he was an expert rider and cared for the family herds. Brothers and friends practiced marksmanship; and in their early teens they hunted buffalo calves together. In their late teens they were allowed to join war parties, and to do chores for the adult warriors. Friends would try to join the same military society so they could fight together, and if necessary, die together.

There were no elaborate rituals for initiating an Indian boy into manhood. He simply took his place when he showed he was ready. He would then begin courting a girl, although he probably would not marry until he owned some horses. If he was wealthy, he might have more than one wife.

By the time he was forty, he no longer went on war parties, but joined the council of the elders, whose advice was asked and respected by all.

Plains Indians did not often display their emotions, but the death of a brave warrior brought scenes of open grief, with close friends and relatives often gashing their bodies as a sign of mourning.

A tattooed Cree Indian chief. Dreams told the wearer what shape the design should take.

Plains Indian Shield Ceremony. "A young man arrived at the age to take his place among the ranks of warriors," wrote George Catlin, "requires a shield, which he makes of the skin of the buffalo's neck." As the shield hardened over a slow fire, friends and warriors danced about it, singing sacred songs.

Carl Bodmer made this picture of a Plains Indian Scalp Dance. When warriors returned from battle with enemy scalps, the bloody trophies were often stretched on hoops, and then attached to long poles. As the men sang of their brave deeds, the women formed a circle and held the scalps aloft, as they danced.

Indian boys began to ride horses almost as soon as they learned to walk. As they grew older, the men of the tribe—as shown here—would allow them to help break in the wild ponies captured on the Plains. Young men hoped to own many, as wealth was counted in terms of horses. The Sioux valued horses greatly, speaking of them as sunka wakan (mystery dogs) and considered them to be sacred.

When a brave died, his women placed his body in the crotch of a tree, or on a scaffold, as shown above. Relatives watched beside him, howling in grief. Often his horse was sacrificed, or its mane cropped short in mourning.

49

ARTS OF THE PLAINS INDIAN

This rare specimen of Sioux woodcarving is a ceremonial club, used in the Horse Dance.

As nomads, the Plains tribes did not like to carry anything but the essentials of daily living. As a result, only the village tribes developed pottery or basket-weaving. Except for ceremonial stone pipes, they rarely carved in wood or stone. But their buffalo robes and tepees were brightly painted with pictures, and their parfleches and cases for medicine bundles were often covered with vivid geometric patterns.

Men usually decorated robes with a record of their military exploits. In these paintings a line sometimes stood for a man, and a semicircle for a horse; but sometimes figures were quite realistic.

Arikara basket. Village Indians wove carrying-baskets meant to be worn on the back. Leather strap circled the wearer's forehead.

Porcupine quillwork of the Plains Indians: (top row) an Arapaho disk, used as a tepee ornament, 1880; a narrow strip of Mandan design, collected by George Catlin in 1831; and a Sioux tobacco pouch, 1890. In the center are a Sioux knife sheath, 1850; and a Sioux quill pouch, 1850, made of an elk bladder. The wide shoulder band, (bottom row) was made by the Sioux in 1860. Indian women dyed the quills with roots and berries, and then sewed them onto soft leather hides. Vegetable dyes were paler than the bright chemical dyes of the white traders, with which the tobacco pouch (right) is colored.

Plains Indian beadwork: tobacco pouches made in the 1880's by women of the Blackfoot (left), Cheyenne, and Sioux tribes. Beads of shell and bone had long been in use, but after the coming of white traders, glass beads, such as these, became popular as trade items.

Triangles and diamond patterns—sewed with quillwork or beads—were popular with women. Sometimes patterns had meaning, but the meanings varied from tribe to tribe. A cross which meant "star" to an Arapaho might mean "the four quarters of the earth" to a Sioux. Color was meaningful, too. Black might signify "night," or "safe return from battle." Red could mean "thunder," or "sunset," or "blood."

Dyed porcupine quills became much less popular as decoration, after the Indians began to trade with the whites for beads, early in the 1800's.

An Arikara cooking pot, dating from the late 1880's. Almost no pottery was made by the wandering Plains tribes, but it was fairly common among settled village dwellers such as the Arikara, the Hidatsa, and Mandan.

The red stone pipe-bowl (above) was carved by a Sioux sculptor sometime before 1843. Plains Indian painting is seen (right) in a detail from the shirt of Chief Mato-tope, of the Mandans. Mato-tope painted these pictures himself, as they boasted of his deeds in battle. But men left all of the sewing of designs, in the beadwork and in quillwork, to the women.

A Sioux flageolet, or flute, on which a brave would play love songs to his sweetheart.

LIFE OF AN INDIAN WOMAN

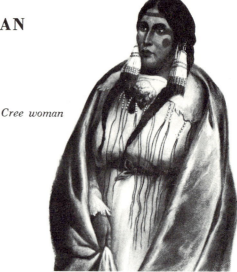

Cree woman

By the time an Indian girl was eight, she would probably find herself in all-female company, rarely seeing even her brothers. Still, an Indian girl's brother was considered her protector. In her growing years she might decorate his moccasins with beadwork, and he might bring her a horse, after a successful raid.

Women had the unglamorous work of making, repairing, and moving the tepees. They hauled wood and water to camp, and dressed the buffalo hides. Young girls learned how to handle these heavy chores before they were married. Marriage to a brave warrior was the height of a girl's ambition.

But despite the drudgery of their lives, women were not looked down upon by male Indians. Nor did a woman feel injured when her husband took another wife—for it would mean that her tasks would be fewer, as her work in camp would now be shared.

Mandan women belonged to a society named the White Buffalo Cow Women. Their magic dance (below) was supposed to cause the buffalo herds to draw near to the Mandan villages.

Indian women curing buffalo hides in a Comanche village in Texas; painted by Catlin in 1834.

An Indian girl takes over the job of minding the baby as her mother gathers firewood.

Dakota Sioux babies, or papooses, might be strapped into cradles like this, hung in the branches of a tree, and rocked to sleep by the wind.

Indian men did the hunting, but only the women took care of the crops. Not all Plains tribes planted gardens, but wild roots and berries were used by all. This group of women is gathering tepia—a wild prairie turnip.

TOMAHAWKS AND SCALPING KNIVES

It is bad to live to be old,
Better to die young
Fighting bravely in battle.

These are the words from a song of the Crazy Dogs, a society of brave young warriors among the Blackfoot Indians. A variation of the song was known to all Plains tribes.

War was the Indian's career and his hobby, his work and his play. With the possible exception of the buffalo hunt, no activity of the Plains Indians was more important than the business of warfare.

They frequently fought to preserve their hunting grounds or to capture horses. Yet they did not go

to war chiefly to kill enemies, or to capture slaves. As nomads, they had no need for slaves, and they rarely took prisoners.

Tribe ruthlessly massacred neighboring tribe. Enemies were often scalped, tortured, and killed in pure revenge. But among most of the Plains tribes, such actions did not rate as highly as did deeds of valor.

For amid all the ceremony, all the preparation of dress and weapons, and the prayers, one startling thing stands out: Plains Indians never went into battle without the hope of winning personal glory.

When the Indian warrior dashed up to a live enemy, near enough to touch him with his hand, a stick, or a lance, he had reached the height of bravery. Compared to this, killing or scalping an enemy required less courage. After all, a skilled archer could shoot a man from a distance and never bring himself close to danger. The scalping of a dead enemy did not involve personal risk, and, besides, the man might have been killed by another warrior.

The striking of a live enemy was called *coup*, from the French word meaning "hit" or "strike." Special sticks with which to touch the enemy were called coup sticks.

Such importance was attached to the counting of coup that few men dared to lie about their achievements. Men caught in such a lie would be shunned, and in some cases, severely punished. The strict rules of Plains Indian warfare are shown in the way they counted coup. The Assiniboin tribe believed that "killing an enemy counts nothing unless his person is touched or struck." They did, however, allow up to four men to count coup on the same enemy. First ranking went to

"The Captive Charger" by Wimar shows a band of Plains Indians making off with a United States cavalryman's horse.

Plains Indians often took enemy scalps, but the victims sometimes survived.

what each deed of bravery was worth. Cheyenne children imitated their elders in nearly all their games. After a mock war was ended, and the children's recital of coup began, another youngster was chosen to judge the actual worth of their deeds.

A warrior who exposed himself while killing an enemy ranked higher than one who killed while hidden. It was thought braver to kill with a lance or a club than to kill from a distance with a gun or bow and arrow. Competition for coup honors was very great. Sometimes a man who killed an enemy from a distance would find that before he could reach his victim, one or more of his comrades had scalped him or taken his shield. They would be awarded higher honors than the actual killer.

the man who struck him while he was alive. After that, lesser honors would be given to those who killed him or scalped him.

The Crow and the Arapaho also allowed four men to count coup on a single enemy, but the Cheyenne permitted only three. The rules were so firmly fixed among the tribes that men knew from childhood exactly

Every deed of daring had a definite value attached to it, although these varied from tribe to tribe. With few exceptions, all tribes graded the deed according to the amount of courage it took to carry it out. Among the Blackfoot, the taking of an enemy's gun was given the highest ranking. Just behind it came the taking of an enemy's shirt, bonnet, or shield. So highly did the Blackfoot rate the taking of a gun that the

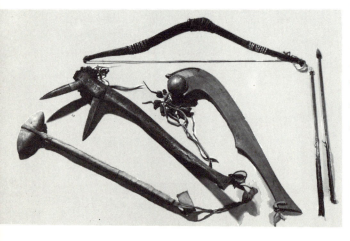

Until trade began with white men, the Indians had no steel. Clubs were made of stone (left), antlers (center), or wood. Arrows were tipped with stone.

56

word for war honor in the Blackfoot language, *namachkani*, means "a gun taken."

On the other hand, the Blackfoot did not give much credit for the seizure of an enemy's horse, while among other tribes this ranked nearly as high as striking a live enemy. The Blackfoot took it for granted that by the time their men were warriors they would have learned how to be expert horse raiders.

Receiving a wound in battle earned some recognition, but among the Crow, the rescue of a wounded comrade was ranked higher. The leader of a victorious war party, especially if he lost no men, was always honored. This was the only way in which the warriors as a group were glorified.

War parties—especially when the goal was the capture of horses—

Scalps were stretched and dried on hoops and later used as decoration.

were rarely very large. They usually consisted of no more than a handful of warriors from a tribe. Later, to defend themselves against

These warriors, back from a successful raid, are "striking the post" with their weapons, and reciting the coups they have counted on their enemies.

A war party (above) moves in "Indian file." (Below) Assiniboin Indians begin
a surprise attack on a Blackfoot camp pitched outside of Ft. McKenzie, a
fur-trading post in Montana. Bodmer saw the battle, from the fort, in 1833.

American soldiers, entire tribes, or even two or more tribes together, formed huge armies to attack the enemy. Even so, individual bravery and coup kept their importance.

The weapons of the Plains Indian were ideal for mounted warfare. The bows were only about three feet long, for easier handling on a horse. A quiver could carry up to 100 arrows which were a little more than two feet long. An arrow was a silent weapon which did not reveal the position of a hidden archer. An Indian could reach his arrows, fit them to the bow, aim, and shoot so fast that several would be in the air at one time. Catlin once saw the Mandans play a game in which they tried to see who could keep the most arrows in the air. Some of the Indians had as many as eight in flight at once. Before repeating rifles came into use, many Indians preferred their bows, as they could be fired faster than the earlier muzzle-loading flintlock muskets.

Some Indians went into battle with clubs and lances as well as bows and arrows. But as with all other things in Plains Indian warfare, there were rules; among the Comanches, only experienced fighters were allowed to carry lances.

Plains Indians preferred the surprise attack; it was sometimes made after dark, but usually at dawn. When surprised and put on the defensive, Indians were generally poor fighters. They tended to scatter and run. Defensive warfare interested them so little that Indian camps were rarely guarded at night. This made them easy targets for their enemies. Later, white soldiers learned this habit of the Indians, and

A Scalp Dance, performed by a Sioux war society, after return from battle.

won many victories with surprise dawn attacks of their own.

But in attack, the Indian was terrifying. He would push his horse to great speed and come swooping down on the enemy camp. A brave chief would form the war party and lead it on its first assault. But after that it was every man for himself.

The use of one or more decoys to lure an enemy into ambush was a favorite Indian trick. It called for great skill on the part of the man chosen as the decoy. Once, in the 1820's, a band of Cheyenne camped near the North Platte River. It was soon after a battle in which they had killed many Crow and had taken a number of prisoners. From their camp the Cheyenne saw a lone man riding back and forth on a nearby hill. Women who went to gather water and wood reported that he was singing sadly, as if in mourning. The men thought he must be a Crow and suspected trouble. Orders went out that no one was to go near him until a large war party was ready.

But twelve Cheyenne, eager for glory, mounted their horses and rode toward the man. Soon after, the other Cheyenne warriors rode out as well, but they were some distance behind the original twelve. The Indian on the hill saw the first group and rode slowly away. The Cheyenne approached close enough to see that he really was a Crow.

Then as he rode faster, the Cheyenne gave chase. When the Crow rode between a gap in the hills, the Cheyenne swiftly followed. And as they, too, passed through the gap, from the sides of the hills hordes of Crow fighters came howling and swooping down on them. The main body of Cheyenne, who had followed the first twelve, saw the rising dust of battle and knew at once what had happened. They dashed to the fight and drove off the Crow warriors, killing six. But of the twelve Cheyenne who first followed the decoy, eight were dead.

After a battle, no Plains Indian made a secret of his bravery. In fact, he was expected to make a public showing of his courage. A young man was usually a member of a military tribal society, and he acted out his battle feats before his comrades. At large ceremonies he would perform before the whole tribe.

He decorated the cover of his tepee with pictures inspired by dreams and visions, or with painted records of his military glory. More often he would paint a single buffalo skin with the story of his greatest coups. The pictures were always simple and direct, sometimes merely outlines of the human beings, horses, and weapons.

Sometimes great pains were taken to show exact detail of dress, shields, and bonnets. At other times, symbols were used, such as horse tracks, which stood for horses.

Nor were pictures the only public display of a man's bravery. In nearly every tribe, there were recognized marks which men could carry with them at all times, very much like the medals given to courageous soldiers and sailors. Feathers or scalps on a coup stick told all who saw them how often their owner distinguished himself in battle. Usually one coup merited one feather. After the Battle of Little Big Horn, Chief Crazy Horse's coup stick carried eleven feathers.

Some tribes wore animal tails, skins, and hair as their version of medals. The Crow tied wolf tails to their moccasins. Deer tails were worn by some tribes, locks of hair from enemy scalps by others.

Once, among the Cheyenne, a warrior exiled for a wanton murder happened to perform a deed of great daring against the Kiowa. Ordinarily, he would have been awarded the highest honors for the coups he counted that day. But under the code of the Cheyenne, as an exile from the tribe, he was allowed to wear no mark of his achievement. Nor was his exile ended.

Although the Plains Indians looked forward to warfare with pleasure and excitement, they always prepared for it with rituals.

A Crow warrior and his horse, wearing war bonnets and full-dress battle array.

Arikara shield. Its owner believed the design gave him magic power in battle.

Many Indians would not go off to war unless the "signs" were favorable. The signs might come in a dream or a vision. Sometimes they told the warrior where and when to fight; sometimes they foretold his luck in battle.

Many a brave warrior refused to join a war party because the signs in a dream warned him to remain at home. His word was never questioned; and his refusal to go into battle, in such cases, was never considered an act of cowardice. But a man turning back from a war party without a sign, was scorned.

Visions and dreams also indicated the kind of design that should be painted on a war shield. The shield had no "protective medicine" until the proper design—usually a symbolic version of the dream—was painted on it.

Shield covers were also symbolically decorated. A shield was a sacred object, and was not removed from its cover until just before battle. Shield and cover were usually buried with their owner at his death, unless he had passed them on to a younger brave warrior. The shield, made from the tough neck and breast skin of the bull buffalo, was protection against arrows but could not turn direct rifle fire. Even so, the Indians firmly believed in the power of the shield's design, and felt that a wound was due to "bad medicine" and not to a faulty shield.

Before going to war, the Plains Indians often painted their faces and bodies as well as their war horses. These designs, too, were revealed in dreams. Red was the most popular color for body painting because it meant strength. (The use of red paint by all the Indian tribes caused them to be spoken of as "red men" and "redskins" by early white explorers. Actually, the color of Indians' skins varies from nearly white to deep brown.)

On returning from success in battle—especially after an enemy had been killed—black was the color most favored. Men who had performed bravely would blacken their faces and march around the camp with the prizes they had snatched.

Eagle feathers, worn by the Sioux, told a story. Braves wearing feather (1) had killed an enemy; (2, 7) cut an enemy's throat; (3, 4, 5) had been the third, fourth, or fifth to strike the enemy; while the wearer of (6) had himself been wounded.

No Plains Indian warrior started fighting without offering a special prayer for success. Often he prayed to the sun or to the moon. Sometimes he would promise to torture himself in a tribal dance or to give something valuable to others in the tribe.

Then, to help those awful moments which come to everyone before the start of combat, he would chant a favorite war song—one of his own or one popular with the military society to which he belonged. And its words would help him to arouse that courage which made him so deadly in battle.

I am a Fox
I am supposed to die.
If there is anything difficult,
If there is anything dangerous,
That is mine to do.

After white traders began supplying steel knives, arrowheads, and axes to the Plains Indians in the 1800's, weapons became still more deadly. (See page 56.)

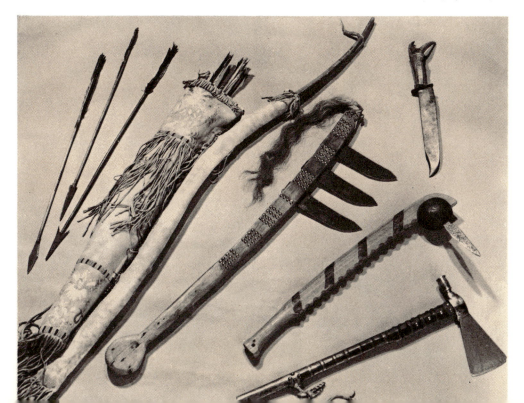

GOOD MEDICINE

The Plains Indians believed in invisible spirits who sent them dreams, visions, and magical signs. The spirits sent them to bring the Indians success and wealth, to ward off misfortune, and to foretell the future. Living close to nature, whose tricks and whims and changes often came suddenly and always without explanation, the Plains Indians had to look to guardian spirits for answers.

The comings and goings of the buffalo herds were irregular. Periods of plenty were followed by periods of scarcity. What was easier to believe, as the Teton-Dakota believed, than that somewhere there was a "Great Unseen Buffalo" who controlled the movements of all the earth's buffaloes? Or that death in battle could be prevented, by rites performed over a bundle of sacred objects—even if the objects were only a pipe, tobacco, some grains of corn, and a feather? Or that the gods would respect a man who fasted and tortured himself?

This trust in supernatural magic was given many names by the Indians. The white man has lumped their beliefs together under the word "medicine." The Indians gave this word many meanings. It often meant a thing, or a method, used to

The Okipa or
Torture Ceremony of the Mandans.

cure illness or disease. But there was also "good medicine" which had the power to prevent harm, and "bad medicine," which brought illness, bad luck, even death.

Indians sometimes made their own medicine bundles, the contents

64

Sun Dances of other tribes featured like tortures.

of which were dictated by dreams and visions. But they often borrowed or bought good medicine from owners whose personal glory and success was proof of their medicine's powers. Whole tribes had medicine bundles which were treated as sacred objects, and which were supposed to protect the entire group.

Among the Arapaho, a flat pipe was wrapped in many layers of cloth and kept in a special, painted tepee guarded by a special keeper. One of his duties was to see that the

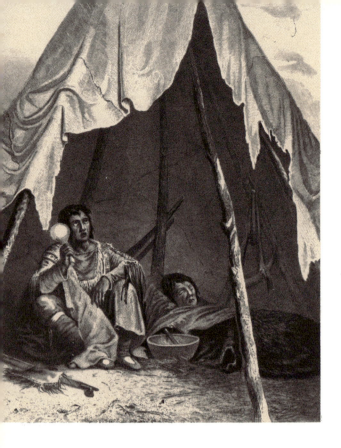

Otherwise, the favors which they asked would not be granted.

Before beginning ceremonies in which sacred objects were used, or before seeking a vision, the Plains Indians often took part in a purification ritual. This consisted of sweating, in a lodge especially built for the purpose. The lodge was a small domed structure made of arched willows, covered with buffalo robes. There was a fireplace in the center into which red-hot rocks were placed. Water was then poured on the rocks, which sent up billows of steam and caused the man in the lodge to sweat.

The steaming-sweating process was carried out a number of times. After the last sweating, the Indian would plunge into a nearby stream in summer, or into a snowbank in winter. Thus purified, he was ready to make an offering or seek a vision.

Visions were the key to the religion of the Plains Indians. To bring on a vision, an Indian would leave his tribe and go off alone to spend days without food or water.

Young men were expected to seek visions. They looked for some quiet spot—the top of a mountain or hill, or a peaceful lakeside—and remained there until the vision came.

A supernatural animal or bird, or a power of nature such as thunder might appear to him in human form

pipe bundle was properly hung, because it was believed that bad luck would follow if it ever touched the ground. The keeper was also charged with repeating the Arapaho legend of the pipe's origins. He took three nights to tell the story.

The pipe was supposed to have been given to the first Arapaho soon after the world began—that is, after the Turtle had brought the Earth up from under the Water. The Duck carried the pipe to the Arapaho, and with it brought an ear of corn. It was from the seeds of this ear that all the corn in the world was said to come. Individual Arapahos seeking favors made offerings to the pipe and had to follow strictly defined rules on the way it was to be held.

and speak to him in his own language. It would take pity on him and offer to give him some of its power. It instructed him how to make up his medicine, which was a token of that power.

Whatever the Indian saw had a meaning, or could be given a meaning, to guide his future actions. And from his visions would come the designs painted on war shields and tepees, his songs to ward off death in warfare, and his cures for illnesses.

Unfortunately, there were Indians to whom visions would not come, no matter how hard they tried. But the Indians solved that problem in a simple manner. A successful man, who owned many horses or who had proved himself in warfare was permitted to sell part of his good medicine to others.

Even those who already had good medicine of their own sometimes sought to buy more. For a price (usually one or more horses), the successful man would sell his own medicine bundle.

Once he had his good medicine, a Plains Indian could count on its lasting protection unless he performed some forbidden act, or taboo. In that case, to restore strength to his medicine, he might have to go through another purification. Occasionally, he would also take part in a Sun Dance as well. And if nothing brought back his lost power, he could seek a new vision and create new medicine.

Blackfoot headdresses worn by a female Sun Dancer (top) and a medicine man.

A Mandan rain maker begs the spirits to send showers to the dry cornfields.

Very different from the lonely vigil was the mass tribal ceremony. Nothing joined the Plains Indians together more strongly than the Sun Dance. Its name comes from the Sioux, who called it the "Sun-gazing Dance." Nearly all the Plains tribes celebrated it, although its form varied from tribe to tribe. For some, the Sun Dance assured the arrival of buffaloes for the fall hunt, and was performed in late summer.

Often it celebrated the coming together of the tribe after the winter's separation. Sometimes it was danced to protect the tribe from its enemies. It often contained acts of self-torture by young warriors asking for favors, or seeking to repay the gods for past gifts. An eye-witness account by an American army officer describes the Sun Dance as follows:

"Those who were to dance only had for clothing a wrapping about their loins; sometimes, I was told, they only wore a breech-cloth. They each had an attendant, who painted him, filled his pipe, rubbed the palms of his hands with sage and other green herbs, and talked encouragingly to him. They seemed to need the encouragement, for they were faint and weak from fasting.

"Around them were feasting and laughter. The circular shed was filled with people, who had brought huge kettles of food. Later the women kinsfolk, wives, sisters and sweethearts, came in singing and had their arms slashed by the medicine man's knife, thus endeavoring to support with their suffering the pain and the torture being undergone by the men.

"Finally one of the dancers was laid with his head near the foot of

"Blackfoot Pipe Stem Carrier," by Paul Kane, shows a medicine man holding a gorgeously-feathered, sacred medicine pipe, which protected the tribe from evil.

Mandans arranged the skulls of men and buffaloes in magic circles on the Plains.

the Sun Dance pole, and two holes were cut in the muscles of his chest, through which two sticks or skewews were thrust. To each of these sticks a string was fastened; then the victim was lifted up, and the strings were fastened to a lariat hanging from the pole. The victim now blew on a whistle made from the bone of an eagle's wing, looked at the sun and its course from its rising to its setting, and until he could free himself by tearing out the flesh and muscles, dancing, whistling, praying for deliverance, and making other requests."

Until late in the nineteenth century, when the Ghost Dance swept the Plains tribes, the Sun Dance was the most important mass religious ceremony of the Indians. And it was their largest social event as well. For while it was held, military societies held their meetings, old friendships were renewed, women were courted, and games were played.

Other dances of the Plains Indians were not directly connected with belief in the supernatural, although some of them did have religious features. Many of the military societies had elaborate dance ceremonies to entertain the tribal reunions.

War dances were meant to whip up enthusiasm for battle rather than to bring about victory. If the fight was successful there would often be a victory dance afterward. Women frequently held dances of their own before battles to insure the success-

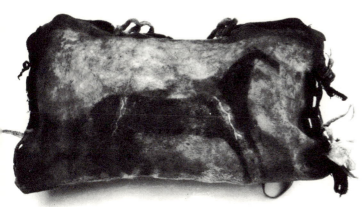

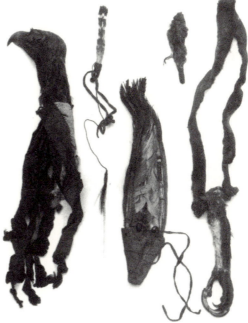

Crow Indians made medicine bundles to give themselves magic power in battle. The painted cover (left) might contain the head and claw of an eagle, fur, and feathers (below).

ful return of their husbands. After battle, men and women conducted scalp dances in which the women put the scalps, taken by their warriors, on long poles and carried them about the camp.

During serious illness, a tribal medicine man, or shaman, might perform a dance about his patient. The shaman's chief duty was to cure the sick, a power he received from the spirit world. The shaman often claimed other powers, and worked many tricks to prove them, but it was largely as a healer that he gained his standing in the tribe.

Sometimes a shaman had only a single medical skill, such as the ability to treat arrow wounds or snake bites. Many performed feats of sleight of hand when treating the ill. Observers would swear they saw the shaman remove insects, stones, or bones from a sick person's body, and thus bring about his recovery.

If a patient did not respond to treatment by a shaman, or if he died, it was usually considered the patient's fault. He had perhaps vio-

lated a taboo or he had not followed the shaman's instructions exactly.

In sickness and in health, the supernatural had as much meaning for the Plains Indian as did the actual world around him. It supplied him with answers to nature's mysteries. But most of all, it gave him the faith he needed to sustain him on the battlefield, on the hunting grounds and, at last, on the hated reservations.

THE COMING OF THE WHITE MEN

For 250 years after Coronado's expedition, as the Plains Indians developed their customs and sharpened their skills of fighting and hunting and riding, very few white men ventured into their land.

Those who came after the retreat of Coronado and his army found the Great Plains just as cruel a land as he had found it. They clung to the dream of fabled cities for many years. But the Plains tribes were hostile and the Spanish found it easier to leave them alone, as a buffer to the French and English to the north and east.

In 1866, pioneer artist William H. Jackson painted a wagon train crossing the South Platte. Wagons were made with watertight bottoms for fording rivers.

At last the Spaniards gave up hunting for gold in favor of establishing missions and ranches in the Southwest. From Canada, the French and English came to trade for furs, but they had no desire to settle on the Plains. Nearly all who entered the broad Plains came back with the same conclusion reached by the first visitors. The country belonged to the Indian and the buffalo. No one else would ever be able to live there.

And so the image grew. West of the Mississippi River, stretching to the foot of the Rocky Mountains, and from the Canadian border to deep into Texas, lay an apparently unconquerable world.

The breaking of the image started with the purchase of the Louisiana Territory by President Thomas Jefferson in 1803. The land was uncharted then, and unexplored except by a very few white men. It was considered the "unknown and the unknowable" in 1804 when Jefferson sent Captain Meriwether Lewis and Captain William Clark to explore "the interior parts of North America." Lewis and Clark came back after an expedition of more than two years. Their journey had taken them beyond the Plains to the Pacific Ocean. They and their men were received as heroes in the East when they returned.

Not many were adventurous enough to follow their trail across the Plains. Most of those who sought the great Northwest, described by Lewis and Clark, went by sea.

Lewis and Clark held a council with Missouri and Oto Indians in 1804.

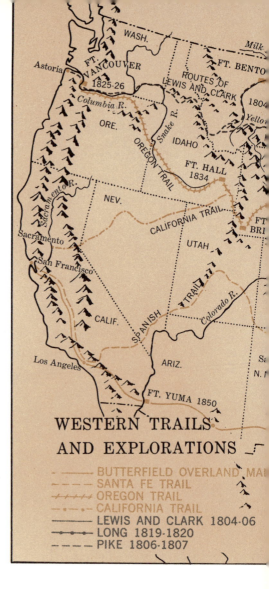

WESTERN TRAILS AND EXPLORATIONS

- ········· BUTTERFIELD OVERLAND MAIL
- ─ ─ ─ SANTA FE TRAIL
- ┼┼┼┼ OREGON TRAIL
- ─·─·─ CALIFORNIA TRAIL
- ────── LEWIS AND CLARK 1804-06
- ●─●─● LONG 1819-1820
- ─ ─ ─ PIKE 1806-1807

Explorers after Lewis and Clark had equally wondrous things to report, but very few good words for the Plains. In 1806, Lieutenant Zebulon M. Pike crossed Kansas to Colorado before going south. He discovered a mountain peak which today carries his name, although at the time he thought it could not be climbed. His words echoed Coronado's: the Plains were "incapable of cultivation," he said, and should be left "to the wandering and uncivilized aborigines of the country."

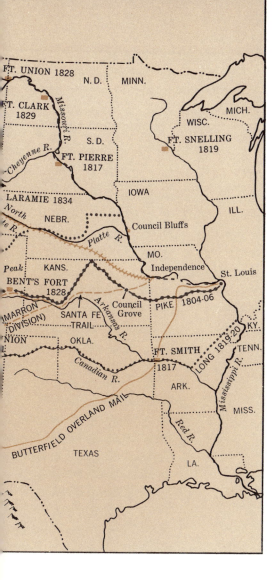

ies was identified as desert land in keeping with Long's description. On all maps the area was left blank. Newspapers spoke of it as a mysterious unknown.

The reports of Pike and Long influenced official United States policy. Beyond the first row of states west of the Mississippi a so-called permanent Indian frontier was established. It was unlikely, government officials thought, that any whites would ever want to settle there. Between 1825 and 1840 many Indian tribes from east of the Mississippi were removed to these lands. Treaties were made with the Plains tribes to permit this resettlement. Companies of dragoons (mounted riflemen) marched on the Plains to impress the Indians and keep them peaceful. As late as 1841, George Catlin suggested that the Plains be made a "national park" to preserve both the Indians and the buffalo.

But if no one chose to live in the

A Blackfoot was killed by Lewis during the expedition's return journey.

From 1819 to 1820 an expedition under Major Stephen H. Long made a similar journey. Like the others, Long said the Plains were "wholly unfit for cultivation."

Long was the first to call the Plains "The Great American Desert," a name and an idea which persisted in this country until after the Civil War. Long saw the scarcity of wood and water as an "insuperable obstacle" to settlement. In schoolbooks of those years, the space between the Mississippi and the Rock-

empty space, many persons had to pass through it—although after 1834 they needed a government permit to do so. Following the Lewis and Clark report, there came men who sought in the Rockies and the far Northwest the beavers whose fur was fashionable, and therefore valuable, back East.

They were the fur trappers, the mountain men—John Colter, who had been with Lewis and Clark, Kit Carson, Tom Fitzpatrick, Jim Bridger, and Jed Smith—and they came to know the Great Plains better than any white men before them.

By 1830 there were some 600 white trappers out West. By then trading posts had been established and the Plains Indian started to meet more white men than he had ever seen.

The Indians trapped the beavers and brought their pelts to the trading posts built by the fur companies. Some posts became famous—Bent's Fort, Fort Union, Fort Laramie. Trading posts also accepted buffalo hides in exchange for cloth and whiskey and guns.

There were 150 trading posts west of the Mississippi in the 1840's, but

trading posts were not really settlements. The Plains remained merely the land that must be passed through in order to get to California and the Oregon Country. Not until later did the Army buy some of these posts to make them forts to protect the people who stayed on the Plains.

In those years there were three major routes to use to get across the Plains as quickly and as safely as possible. All of them started from a muddy, river-front town called St. Louis. The Santa Fe Trail led to Santa Fe across Kansas and what is now the Oklahoma Panhandle into New Mexico. The Missouri River Route led north and west, up the Missouri River. The Oregon Trail followed the Platte River through Nebraska and Wyoming and led to Oregon's Columbia River valley. Whichever trail men took, they moved as swiftly over the Plains as their transportation and equipment allowed, for dawdling was an invitation to sudden death.

The fear of this "desert," symbolized by these hurrying men, is understandable. The Plains were a new kind of land to men from the East. They and their ancestors were used to forests and mountains and streams. These had been challenges, of course, but challenges that they knew how to meet.

East of the Mississippi, trees could be cut down to build houses, the forests were full of familiar animals to hunt, and there were plenty of fish in the streams. There was a temperate climate which for the most part brought proper amounts of sun and rain to raise crops. Rivers were navigable, the Atlantic Ocean was a link from one coastal city to another—even to Europe itself, from which they or their families had come. In the East, nature seemed to work for man.

But once the Mississippi and Missouri Rivers were crossed, the forests

Plains Indians sometimes attacked emigrant wagon trains on the Oregon Trail.

77

In 1847, a train of Mormons with handcarts crossed the Great Plains to Utah.

were no more, the land was flat. On this dry and treeless plain, the weather could change with startling suddenness. A north wind could cause temperatures to drop 50 degrees in a matter of hours. Hail, of the same dangerous size that Coronado's army had had to endure was always a possibility. Sometimes there were tearing blizzards, in which the wind-driven snow formed drifts as high as houses back East.

And there was the sun, a fierce sun which could bake rivers dry and cause winds to blow hot.

Those who had seen the Plains discouraged those who had not. For most people, the belief that the prairies were a vast desert persisted until the Civil War.

For some, though, the desert image was coming to an end.

Settlers did come to stay in areas later to be called Kansas and Nebraska. And, by the 1840's, the number of men passing through the Plains was increasing. There were fewer and fewer mountain men, and the market for beaver had gone, but the market for buffalo leather had replaced it. Gold was discovered in California, and the men who sought it came overland as well as by ship. Covered wagons brought families to Oregon. Members of a religious sect called the Mormons had walked across the Plains on their way to a promised land now called Utah. Texas had joined the Union, and the war with Mexico which followed (1846–48) sent American troops into many parts of the Southwest.

All of these movements changed men's ideas about the Plains. But there were many who still thought of the Plains as a barren Sahara. The United States Army treated the area as such. Jefferson Davis was Secretary of War from 1853 to 1857 before he became president of the Confederacy. He was a good and an imaginative cabinet officer. He had served with distinction in the Mexican War and knew conditions in the Southwest. As Secretary, he had encouraged surveys for rail routes through the Plains, and had sought ways to irrigate the land. He helped supply army outposts with animals he considered to be highly suitable to the desert—camels!

Davis persuaded Congress to spend $30,000, for the purpose of bringing camels to the army on the southern Plains. An agent purchased the best camels that Smyrna had to offer and by 1857, there were 75 of the hump-backed beasts in service in west Texas and California. But 1857 was also Davis' last year as Secretary of War, and with his departure the Army's interest in camels faded. Nobody knows what happened to the animals. In place of fact, legend has taken hold, and for years tales have been told on the Plains of wild camels roaming the West.

The introduction of camels to the army posts may have been the last attempt at treating the Plains as a desert. Soon after Appomattox, Civil War veterans from north and south started to push beyond the prairie states. Even a desert populated by Indians was no barrier to these land-hungry men. They were beginning to see the Plains as vast farmlands, or as ranges, whose tough grass could support huge herds of cattle or sheep.

The desert myth died, of course, as it had to. Now when the white men came, they brought their wives and children, their herds, their plows and harvesters, and their barbed wire fences. Instead of passing through, they stayed—to build houses, then towns, and cities. They drove the Indian and the buffalo from the Plains.

As Secretary of War, Davis thought camels from Turkey would be useful beasts on "The Great American Desert."

In the early 1800's, men's hats made of beaver fur were so popular that companies were set up in St. Louis, and parties of trappers sent out to the Rocky Mountains to catch the little animal (above). Ashley's newspaper advertisement (below) which appeared on March 20, 1822, in the Missouri Republican, was answered by Jim Bridger and Tom Fitzpatrick.

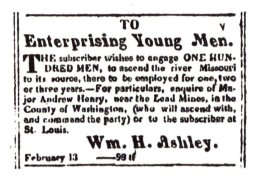

TO
Enterprising Young Men.

THE subscriber wishes to engage ONE HUNDRED MEN, to ascend the river Missouri to its source, there to be employed for one, two or three years.—For particulars, enquire of Major Andrew Henry, near the Lead Mines, in the County of Washington, (who will ascend with, and command the party) or to the subscriber at St. Louis.

Wm. H. Ashley.

February 13 ——98 tf

Kit Carson became a mountain man in 1829, at the age of twenty. He later became one of the most famous Indian scouts in the West.

"The Trappers' Return" shows mountain men returning to camp with a pack of freshly-skinned beaver pelts in their canoe. Once a year, at a rendezvous in Wyoming's Green River valley, they sold their furs.

The trappers—one of whom is shown above—knew the West so well that, after the fur trade declined in the 1840's, many of them became guides and led emigrant trains bound for the Pacific.

MOUNTAIN MEN

Beginning soon after the return of the Lewis and Clark expedition, bands of rough, brave adventurers entered the West to trap beavers in the streams of the Rocky Mountains. William Ashley organized an expedition of 100 men, which his partner, Andrew Henry, led up the Missouri in 1822. These and later parties of trappers, traveling back and forth across the Plains, were among the first Americans to know the Plains Indians.

These pioneers were called "mountain men," and many of their names—Jim Bridger, Tom Fitzpatrick, Kit Carson, John Colter—have become famous.

They roamed huge areas of the West, collecting beaver pelts or "plews" either as free trappers, or as employees of John Jacob Astor's American Fur Company or the Rocky Mountain Fur Company.

After 1840, when the beaver trade was no longer profitable, many veteran mountain men became guides for emigrant trains and parties of explorers, and scouts for the United States Army in Indian country.

Trappers usually got on well with the Indians, but as flatboats traveled down the Missouri, they were occasionally attacked by hostiles.

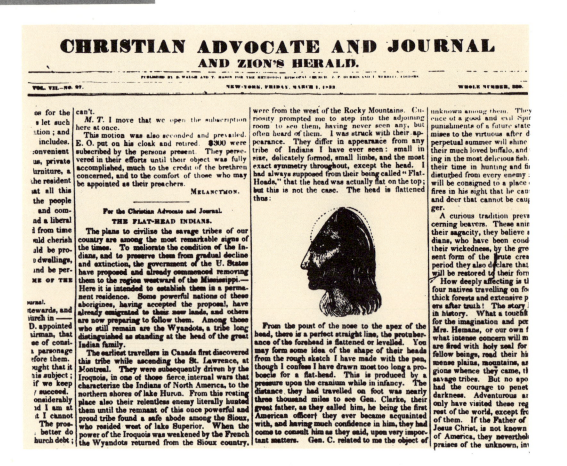

CHRISTIAN ADVOCATE AND JOURNAL
AND ZION'S HERALD.

PUBLISHED BY B. WAUGH AND T. MASON FOR THE METHODIST EPISCOPAL CHURCH. J. P. DURBIN AND T. MERRITT, EDITORS.

VOL. VII.—NO. 27.   NEW-YORK, FRIDAY, MARCH 1, 1833.   WHOLE NUMBER, 350.

...es for the ... let such ...tion; and ...includes. ...convenient ...us, private ...urniture, a ...the resident ...at all this ...the people ...and com... ...d a liberal ...d from time ...uld cherish ...uld be pro... ...e dwellings, ...ind be per... ...ME OF THE

...urnal.

...tewards, and ...urch in —— D. appointed ...airman, that ...ee of consi... ...a parsonage ...efore them. ...ught that it ...his subject; ...if we keep ...y succeed. ...onsiderably ...d I am at ...t I cannot

The pros... ...better do ...hurch debt;

...can't.

M. T. I move that we open the subscription here at once.

This motion was also seconded and prevailed. E. O. put on his cloak and retired. $300 were subscribed by the persons present. They persevered in their efforts until their object was fully accomplished, much to the credit of the brethren concerned, and to the comfort of those who may be appointed as their preachers.

MELANCTHON.

For the Christian Advocate and Journal.
THE FLAT-HEAD INDIANS.

The plans to civilize the savage tribes of our country are among the most remarkable signs of the times. To meliorate the condition of the Indians, and to preserve them from gradual decline and extinction, the government of the U. States have proposed and already commenced removing them to the region westward of the Mississippi.— Here it is intended to establish them in a permanent residence. Some powerful nations of these aborigines, having accepted the proposal, have already emigrated to their new lands, and others are now preparing to follow them. Among those who still remain are the Wyandots, a tribe long distinguished as standing at the head of the great Indian family.

The earliest travellers in Canada first discovered this tribe while ascending the St. Lawrence, at Montreal. They were subsequently driven by the Iroquois, in one of those fierce internal wars that characterize the Indians of North America, to the northern shores of lake Huron. From this resting place also their relentless enemy literally hunted them until the remnant of this once powerful and proud tribe found a safe abode among the Sioux, who resided west of lake Superior. When the power of the Iroquois was weakened by the French the Wyandots returned from the Sioux country.

were from the west of the Rocky Mountains. Curiosity prompted me to step into the adjoining room to see them, having never seen any, but often heard of them. I was struck with their appearance. They differ in appearance from any tribe of Indians I have ever seen: small in size, delicately formed, small limbs, and the most exact symmetry throughout, except the head. I had always supposed from their being called "Flat-Heads," that the head was actually flat on the top; but this is not the case. The head is flattened thus:

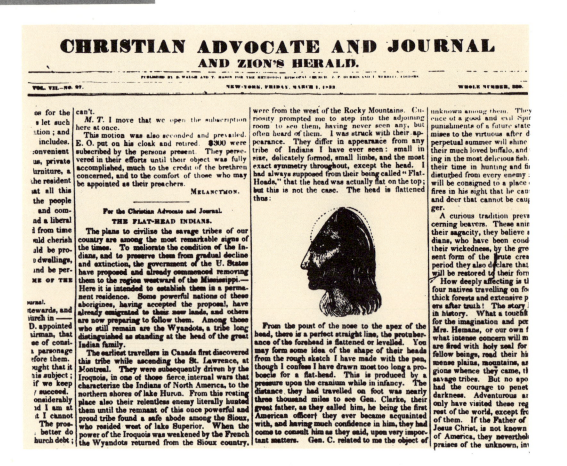

From the point of the nose to the apex of the head, there is a perfect straight line, the protuberance of the forehead is flattened or levelled. You may form some idea of the shape of their heads from the rough sketch I have made with the pen, though I confess I have drawn most too long a proboscis for a flat-head. This is produced by a pressure upon the cranium while in infancy. The distance they had travelled on foot was nearly three thousand miles to see Gen. Clarke, their great father, as they called him, he being the first American officer they ever became acquainted with, and having much confidence in him, they had come to consult him as they said, upon very important matters. Gen. C. related to me the object of

unknown among them. They ...ence of a good and evil Spir... punishments of a future state... mises to the virtuous after d... perpetual summer will shine... their much loved buffalo, and... ing in the most delicious fish... their time in hunting and fi... disturbed from every enemy: ... will be consigned to a place... fires in his sight that he can... and deer that cannot be caug... ger.

A curious tradition preva... cerning beavers. These anim... their sagacity, they believe... dians, who have been cond... their wickedness, by the gre... sent form of the brute crea... period they also declare that... will be restored to their form

How deeply affecting is t... four natives travelling on fo... thick forests and extensive p... ers after truth! The story... in history. What a touchi... for the imagination and po... Mrs. Hemans, or our own f... are fired with holy zeal for... fellow beings, read their hi... mense plains, mountains, a... gions whence they came, t... savage tribes. But no apo... had the courage to penet... darkness. Adventurous a... only have visited these reg... rest of the world, except fr... of them. If the Father of... Jesus Christ, is not known... of America, they nevertho... praises of the unknown, in...

On March 1, 1833, a Methodist newspaper—The Christian Advocate and Journal—printed this article. It told of four Flathead Indians who had journeyed from Oregon to St. Louis, seeking instruction in the white man's religion for their tribe. Their story so moved Jason Lee, Marcus Whitman, and other Protestant ministers that expeditions were sent out to Oregon. In 1836, Marcus Whitman and his wife Narcissa set up a mission among the Cayuse Indians in Washington. But in 1847 (below) the Cayuses murdered them.

Father de Smet was beloved by the Blackfoot, who called him "Black Robe." In 1840, they met him in front of their village, sat him on a buffalo robe, and carried him in state to their chief.

EARLY MISSIONARIES

Very few white men were more completely trusted by the Plains Indians than the missionary priest, Father Pierre-Jean de Smet. A Jesuit who first came to the upper Missouri River in 1840, he devoted his life to ministering to the Indians. He spent most of his working life among the Flatheads of the northwest.

A few years prior to Father de Smet's arrival, Protestant missionaries had crossed the Plains on their way to Oregon. To these missionaries—such as Jason and Daniel Lee who crossed the Plains in 1834, and to Samuel Parker and Marcus Whitman a year later—goes credit for being the first pioneers of the West to know the Plains Indians, after the trappers and traders.

In 1871, a Jesuit priest, Father Lacombe, drew this picture chart to explain Catholicism to the Blackfoot. On this portion, priests are seen leading their savage charges toward Salvation, away from the black path of Evil.

Indians of the Plains usually welcomed Christian missionaries as well-meaning friends. But the red man was often quite naturally unwilling to give up his traditional beliefs and ceremonies in favor of the white man's strange, new religion.

In 1868, when Red Cloud was still fighting for the Powder River country, Father de Smet was the only white man the Sioux would permit to enter their lands to negotiate peace.

83

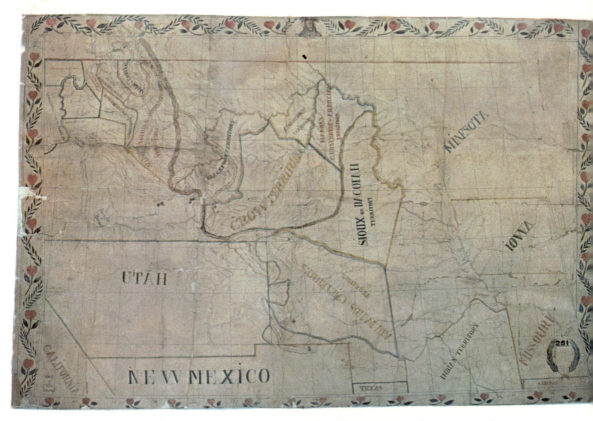

A map of Plains Indian territories, used at the Horse Creek peace conference in 1851, was drawn by the Catholic missionary, Father Pierre-Jean de Smet.

TREATY AND TROUBLE

Horse Creek, a twisting stream in the southeast corner of Wyoming, meets the North Platte River thirty-five miles east of Fort Laramie. There, close to what is now the border of the states of Wyoming and Nebraska, the largest number of American Indians ever gathered in one place pitched their tepees early in September, 1851. No precise count was ever made, but the best estimates are that between eight and ten thousand Indians were camped alongside Horse Creek.

The Indians had gathered for a peace conference, called by the old mountain man Thomas Fitzpatrick. Now he had become government agent for the tribes between the Platte and Arkansas Rivers.

There were the nomadic Sioux, Cheyenne, Arapaho, Crow, Assiniboin and Shoshoni; and from the villages came Hidatsa, Arikara and Mandan. Not far off were the soldiers of Fort Laramie, about 300 men, nervously fingering their guns.

For the truce, which each of the

tribes pledged for the duration of the conference, might easily end in bloody warfare. Hotheads had to be carefully watched, for among the tribes present were many who were lifelong enemies.

The peace conference had been called by the whites to put an end to intertribal warfare and, more important, to put an end to Indian attacks on whites. Washington wanted to be sure that people going west would be able to travel safely, and it wanted to build forts and military roads in Indian territory.

In return for this, the government officials were prepared to establish definite boundaries for the tribes within which they could hunt and roam freely. They would also protect the Indians against white attacks and promised to punish offenders. In addition the Indians were to receive an annual payment of $50,-000 for fifty years.

It sounded fair, at least to officials in Washington who established Indian policy. Unfortunately, these officials had little firsthand information about the Plains tribes. The Indians agreed to the terms laid down by the government commissioners. But there were not many among them who believed the treaty could be made to work.

The Indians had come to the peace conference because they had complaints of their own against the white men. Easterners passing through their hunting grounds had destroyed buffalo herds, trampled the grass, and cut down the few trees. Diseases carried by the white men had killed vast numbers of Indians. In one instance, smallpox had wiped out all but a handful of the Mandan tribe, reducing a community of 1600 people to about 150 who went to live with the Hidatsa.

Cholera and measles had taken their toll as well. And to the Indians, who had rarely known disease, it looked as if they were the victims of a special magic known only to the white man. Ruthless traders had introduced liquor to the Indians. Chiefs watched with dismay as they saw braves ruined by whiskey.

The government commissioners did not bring up the chiefs' grievances, even though they were the cause of the Indian attacks on wagon trains going west. Instead, the white man preferred to speak chiefly of the

Father Pierre-Jean de Smet as a young man.

Fort Laramie, as it looked in 1837, when it was a fur-trading post. Two years before the Treaty of Horse Creek, in 1849, Fort Laramie became an army post.

government's right to build roads and forts from which soldiers could protect white travelers.

The commissioners' plans were to fail on two counts. First, the chiefs' signatures on a piece of paper would not be enough to end feuds of long standing between tribes. Second, the Indians would not recognize the authority of the chiefs whom the commissioners named as spokesmen for each of the tribes.

Among the Indians, there were chiefs of small bands, of families, of villages, but no Plains tribe entrusted its leadership to a single chief. Chiefs sometimes set rules for hunts or battles, but the warrior societies saw that they were carried out. Often the society's power was greater than that of a chief.

But the whites insisted on making one man responsible for a tribe. And the Indians calmly accepted the foolishness.

The white commissioners were

wild party, but it could not hide the fact—for the Indians at least—that nothing had been accomplished.

In less than three years' time the feelings between Indian and white were as bad as ever. Second Lieutenant J. L. Grattan, who had been assigned to Fort Laramie fresh from West Point, loudly proclaimed that the Indians were cowards. With ten men he could wipe out all the Cheyenne, he said, and with thirty he could defeat all the Plains Indians.

In the summer of 1854, Grattan got his chance. A sickly cow had been abandoned by a Mormon emigrant. A Sioux of the Miniconjou band, in need of rawhide, simply killed the animal and stripped what he needed from its back. The Mormon complained at the fort, hoping to collect money for the dead cow.

Bear-That-Scatters, chief of the

enthusiastic when the treaty was signed. One officer called the treaty "the best that could have been made for both parties." To celebrate, the whites brought out gifts for all the Indians present. The chiefs received beef and bacon, coffee and kettles, thread and cloth, medals and uniforms. There were knives and brass buttons for the young men. It was a

The interior of Fort Laramie, Wyoming.

Indians traded furs, at trading posts such as this, for kettles, guns, and tobacco.

Brûlé band of the Sioux (the man whom the whites had named leader of all the Sioux) said he would help bring in the Indian culprit.

Lieutenant H. B. Fleming, then in charge of the fort, did not think the problem very serious. He was willing to leave it to the Indian agent. But to Grattan this seemed the time to make his reputation as an Indian fighter. He insisted that he be allowed to bring back the guilty Indian. Fleming agreed, but knowing of Grattan's boasts, he ordered him to take the Indian only "if practicable and without unnecessary risks."

Grattan called for volunteers "for dangerous service," raised a total of thirty men, and equipped himself with two howitzers. He marched out of the fort announcing that he would "conquer or die." His small band marched the nine miles between the fort and the Sioux camps where the Oglala, Miniconjou, and Brûlé bands had set up their tepees near a trading post. Grattan halted a few yards from the Miniconjou lodges and while his detail set up the howitzers, he walked to the Indian camp. Two chiefs, Bear-That-Scatters and Old-Man-Afraid-of-His-Horses, a chief of the Oglala Sioux, came out to meet him. For nearly an

Colonel Harney had fought Indians in Florida and served in the Mexican War.

hour they tried to convince Grattan that payment for the cow would be made as soon as the Indian agent came to the fort.

Grattan returned to his soldiers and, without warning, opened fire on the Indian camp. In the first volley, Bear-That-Scatters was mortally wounded. The Indians leaped to counterattack. As Grattan retreated, he ran directly into a band of Oglalas. Within minutes Grattan and his troops were dead.

Grattan had started the warfare he was so eager to have, and Eastern newspapers reported that the fight was a massacre begun by the Indians. Even the War Department believed the newspapers rather than the men at Fort Laramie, who said that Grattan was to blame.

The next summer, Colonel William S. Harney was assigned to teach the Indians a lesson. Harney marched from Fort Leavenworth to a point on the North Platte River called Ash Hollow. There he found a camp of the Brûlé Indians. Even though their chief, Bear-That-Scatters, had died of the wounds received in the Grattan fight, most of the band were still friendly. But Harney was not there for friendly discussion. He asked that those guilty of the Grattan massacre be surrendered. Little Thunder, a Brûlé chief, realized that Harney was prepared to

fight, and started back to warn his people. At that moment, Harney ordered his troops to attack.

Under fire by cavalry from the left, and infantry from the right, the Indians ran. Harney chased them for five miles, until the Indians were thoroughly scattered. Harney's revenge included eighty-six Indians dead, five wounded, and seventy women and children captured.

From that summer in 1855, the lines were drawn. Except for a handful of chiefs who would cling to the hope that somehow a peaceful solution could be found with the white men, there would be powerful and hostile Plains tribes almost constantly at war with the United States. Each new attack, whether by Indian or white, made matters worse. No one knew when a period of peace would be broken by sudden violence. Battle would follow battle. Not for almost forty years after the Horse Creek Treaty would there be lasting peace on the Plains.

Old-Man-Afraid-of-His-Horses, photographed smoking a pipe at Fort Laramie.

The Santa Fe Trail (above) leading from Independence, Missouri, to Santa Fe, New Mexico, was a most important route into the West. It was used from 1821, when Mexico won her freedom from Spain and permitted Yankee traders to enter her lands, until 1880, when Santa Fe was reached by rail. The most famous route of all, the Oregon Trail, (right) also began in Independence, led to Fort Laramie, crossed the Rockies at South Pass, Wyoming, and ended in Oregon's Columbia River valley. In its peak year, 1847, it was traveled by 4,500 emigrants.

In 1833, Swiss artist Carl Bodmer traveled by steamboat up the Missouri River—a vital route to the West. On his way, he painted this scene of snags in the upper river. By the 1860's steamers were carrying soldiers and gold-seekers to Fort Benton—near present-day Great Falls—as far as steamboats could go.

COVERED WAGONS ON THE PLAINS

In May of 1841, the first emigrant train moved westward along the Platte River. It consisted of a few carts, thirteen wagons, and eighty-one people. It was guided by mountain man Tom Fitzpatrick. The path the emigrants took was to be known as the Oregon Trail to the whites, and as the Great Medicine Road to the Indians.

In 1842, a party of 112 persons crossed the Plains. The next year, a thousand men, women, and children headed west. The Indians thought that this group must be the white's "big village," and that no more would follow.

But soon the Indians saw trains of covered wagons roll past in seemingly endless numbers. Raids on the Conestoga wagons—which became fairly frequent after 1851—did not stop other "ships of the desert" from making the same journey. The emigrant trains continued to roll westward through the 1840's and 1850's.

"Emigrants Attacked by Comanches" shows wagons on the Santa Fe Trail drawn into a circle, fighting off a party of whooping warriors.

Bodmer painted this picture of the steamer Yellowstone *being "cordelled" or towed, in the upper stretches of the swift-flowing Missouri—up to Fort Union on the Dakota border. The men on the bank will inch the steamer forward by pulling on the line attached to its bow. The Remington painting (below), "Downing the Nigh Leader," shows Plains Indians killing one of the lead horses on the overland stage. Stagecoaches took twenty-five days to reach the West Coast from the Missouri.*

SPANNING A CONTINENT

In 1855, the firm of Russells, Majors and Waddell began to operate a freight service to the West Coast. For pioneers needed flour, sugar, bacon, and dry goods, and they wanted mail from home. In a few years the company was operating 6,000 covered wagons pulled by 75,000 oxen. In April, 1860, the same company organized the Pony Express, which could carry a letter from San Francisco to St. Joseph, Missouri in ten days. But eighteen months later, when telegraph service was completed between Missouri and California in October, 1861, the Pony Express went out of business.

A successful mail route to Los Angeles was begun in 1857 by the Butterfield Overland Mail, which also brought passengers out West on stagecoaches. The coming of the railroads—in the 1870's—finished the Overland Mail.

Steamboats—such as the famous *Yellowstone*—carried freight and people up the Missouri, as early as 1832, to Fort Union, near the North Dakota-Montana line. In 1876, even after the coming of railroads to the West, there were still forty-six steamboats on the Great Muddy.

Each of these advances helped the white man establish himself more firmly on the Plains—and each of them was a further threat to the traditional free way of life of the buffalo-hunting Plains Indian.

During their brief year and one-half of service, Pony Express riders (right) traveled 650,000 miles and lost only one pouch of mail. They delivered letters—which had required twenty days to cross the Plains—in half that time.

Fresh horses and riders relieved Pony Expressmen of their mail pouches at stations spaced fifteen miles apart along the way.

93

MASSACRE IN MINNESOTA

The start of the American Civil War brought an uneasy quiet to the frontier towns on the Plains.

Most of the regular army troops were withdrawn from posts in Indian territory. A few Indians could have destroyed those who were left behind. Able Indian agents with Southern sympathies were dismissed from the Indian service. Traders who sided with the South tried to encourage an Indian uprising against Federal troops. Northern newspapers spoke of a Confederate plot to link the Indians with the South.

The Indians had no wish to enter the white man's quarrel. They were happy to be left alone. The reduced number of white soldiers in the West seemed to have a calming effect upon them.

This in itself was a welcome change to both Indians and whites. There had been far too many skirmishes, even though they were small ones. Brave men on both sides had died over trifles.

The Plains Sioux were refused their annual payment in 1857. A band of eastern Sioux, with whom the Plains bands had nothing in common but the name, had (under the leadership of a minor chief named Inkpaduta) massacred the white settlers at Spirit Lake, Iowa. And in 1858, gold was discovered in Colorado. Once more, great numbers of whites—more than 100,000 within the year—trampled over the Indian hunting grounds. To the whites it was "Pike's Peak or Bust." But to the Indian tribes it simply meant that the white man had broken his word once again.

When the Civil War began, many white invaders withdrew from the

94

John Stevens' painting shows the Sioux uprising in Minnesota. A farmer named Myers, who had been kind to the Indians, was spared.

Plains. Most of the gold seekers had gone back home discouraged. The buffalo herds were no longer disturbed. Brave warriors could once again carry on the desperate warfare they understood and loved. Sioux fought Crow, Arapaho fought Ute. To many an Indian it seemed as if the old days had returned.

Then, in Minnesota in 1862, the peace was shattered. The Santee Sioux began a rampage of massacre —the worst in the history of the West. It brought death and destruction to a 200-mile stretch of the frontier. And though the Plains Indians were in no way involved, they were to suffer as well.

On August 23, 1862, the Sioux, under Chief Little Crow, attacked the town of New Ulm, killed farmers harvesting grain in the fields, and then retreated.

There were some whites who tried to understand the cause of the outbreak. General George A. S. Crooker wrote to President Abraham Lincoln from St. Paul, a few weeks after the uprising had been stilled. "I feel confident," he said, "that if all the Indian outbreaks upon this continent were carefully examined and honestly probed to the bottom, the whole cause and origin would be found in the thievish and dishonest conduct of the government agency officers, traders and the vile confederates that procure their appointments and share their plunder and then gloss over and hide their iniquity."

This was an unpopular view. Few men in Minnesota agreed with Crooker, even when the Santee Sioux, under Chief Little Crow, set out to get revenge. The Indians were enraged by the moldy bacon, the wormy flour, and the surpluses in whiskey that private traders always seemed to have. The Indians' own corn crop had been ruined by cutworms; the Santee Sioux were starving and faced the indignity of begging for help from the indifferent white man.

Yet these were Indians whose leader had followed the white man's way. Little Crow had become a convert to Christianity. He was a mem-

Outbuildings were burned in the Sioux assault on Fort Ridgely, Minnesota.

ber of the Episcopal Church fifteen miles from Fort Ridgely, Minnesota. He wore white man's clothes, except for moccasins. He was not ready to blame all whites for the acts of a few agents and traders, or to murder for revenge. But when his tribesmen struck, he was their chief and he would lead them.

August 17, 1862, the day the Minnesota Massacres began, was a Sunday. Little Crow had attended church as usual. It was the last time a friendly word would pass between him and a white man. That afternoon, the Santee Sioux attacked the settlement at Acton. On August 20, Fort Ridgely was besieged, and for six weeks after that, some 2,000 Indians attacked whites wherever they found them.

A woman and child trying to flee in a hay wagon burned to death as the Indians set fire to the hay. In Milford, a township west of New

Ulm, fifty-one people died. An Indian named Cut Nose, who had earned that name after biting off part of an enemy's nose, killed whites "till his arm was tired." Towns were burned, some by the Indians, and some by the whites who chose to burn their homes rather than let the Indians use them as shelter for more shooting.

Traders, especially, came to violent ends. One of them, Andrew J. Myrick, was killed at his own store,

Colonel Sibley had helped bring Minnesota into the Union, as a state, in 1858.

his body mutilated and his mouth stuffed with grass. It was grim Indian humor; just before the massacres began Myrick had been told the Indians were hungry. "Let them eat grass for all I care," he had said.

Ta-oyate-duta.
Little Crow.

Hundreds of women and children were captured by Indians as panic swept the Minnesota farmlands. But Fort Ridgely held, and Little Crow was forced to withdraw. An Indian attack on New Ulm was also driven back, but not before dozens of soldiers were killed.

It was two weeks after the Indian attacks had started before white forces, under Colonel Henry H. Sibley, could regroup and counterattack. And it was three weeks after that before Sibley, with 1600 men, marched toward Little Crow's village on the Yellow Medicine River. There, at Wood Lake, Sibley's men met Little Crow's men. It was a bitter battle, but Sibley's raw recruits held, and finally advanced. The Sioux retreated, then scattered. Sibley had won, but in the confusion of battle, Little Crow escaped.

Sibley captured nearly 2,000 Santee Sioux and rescued most of the surviving white captives. A military commission tried 392 Indians for murder and looting, and 306 were condemned to death. But before the punishment could be carried out, the death sentence was reviewed in Washington. President Abraham Lincoln, worried by severe Union

Little Crow, chief of the Santee Sioux, led the savage uprisings in Minnesota.

98

losses in the Civil War, took time to study the case. Perhaps he was influenced by General Crooker's letter, perhaps by the ruthlessness of the punishment. He commuted the death sentences of all but thirty-eight Indians whose crimes were proven. In 1862, these men were hanged at Mankato, Minnesota.

The hangings did not stop Little Crow. He and his band of fugitives fought on for six months more. Finally, on July 3, 1863, he was killed by white settlers while picking berries near Hutchinson, Minnesota. His scalp, his skull, and his wristbones were put on public exhibition, his body thrown in a waste pile, and many of the men he led moved west to live among the Plains Sioux, where they continued to hope for revenge against the whites.

In Mankato, Minnesota, on December 26, 1862, thirty-eight Santee Sioux, including Cut Nose, were hanged for taking part in the Minnesota Massacres.

BLACK KETTLE AND RED CLOUD

The end of the Civil War brought all-out war to the Plains Indians. Soldiers freed from the eastern battlefields after Appomattox were sent west under battle-trained officers. They were sent to the Plains to protect civilians, to allow them to build homes and farms peacefully on the frontier, and to see that they travelled westward in safety. But the return of the soldiers, and the increased traffic on the hunting grounds led only to fighting.

Even six months before the Civil War ended, some Indians had found that to submit to the whites meant death. Black Kettle, a chief of the Southern Cheyenne, then ranging eastern Colorado, had sought peace.

Despite the gold seekers, who had invaded Indian lands in 1858 and 1859, Black Kettle had told his band that fighting the white man would not solve the Indians' problems. Major E. W. Wynkoop, commandant at Fort Lyon, Colorado, a few miles west of the Kansas line, brought Black Kettle and some other chiefs to a conference. They were to meet J. Evans, governor of the Colorado territory, to try to find a basis for peace. Wynkoop's reward was to be recalled from his post for "violation of orders."

Before he was replaced on November 2, 1864, he assured Black Kettle that the Sand Creek area—thirty miles from Fort Lyon—was a safe

The man in the hat, kneeling in the front row, is Major Wynkoop. Behind him, seated third from left, is Chief Black Kettle of the Cheyenne.

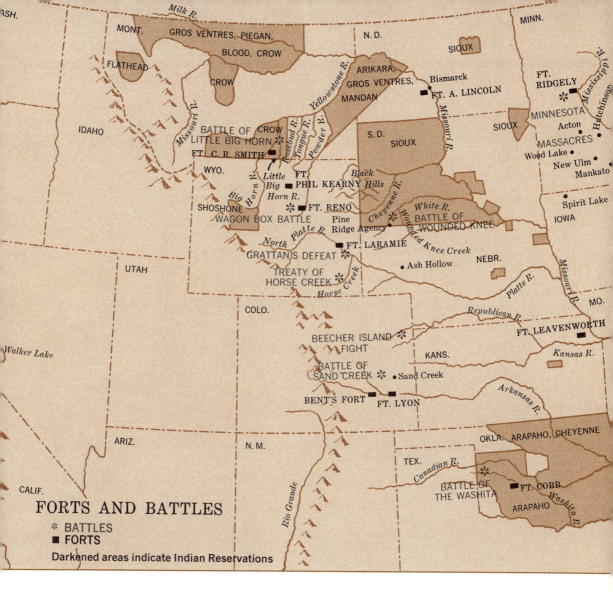

FORTS AND BATTLES

* BATTLES
■ FORTS

Darkened areas indicate Indian Reservations

camping site. There he would be protected by the soldiers as long as his villagers remained peaceful.

Wynkoop's replacement, Major Scott Anthony, repeated this promise of safety to the Indians. In good faith, Black Kettle's camp of Cheyenne—about 100 tepees, and a small band of Arapaho, ten tepees under Chief Left Hand—settled at Sand Creek. About 200 of the 700 people there were warriors; the rest were women, children, and the aged.

Toward the end of November,

Colonel J. M. Chivington, a former minister, arrived at Fort Lyon at the head of six hundred cavalrymen. They were a unit of the Colorado Cavalry—made up of men who had volunteered solely to fight Indians. As soon as Chivington's men arrived, Anthony armed a troop of a hundred men, and marched toward Sand Creek on November 29, 1864.

This legendary anecdote is revealing of Chivington's character:

"The night was bitter cold; Jim [Beckwourth], the old trapper who

had been guiding them . . . turned to [Chivington] and said: 'Wolf he howl. Injun dog he hear wolf, he howl too. Injun he hear dog and listen; hear something, and run off.' The big man [Chivington] tapped the butt of his revolver in an ominous way, and replied: 'Jack, I haven't had an Indian to eat for a long time. If you fool with me, and don't lead us to that camp, I'll have you for breakfast.' They found the camp."

At Sand Creek, sometime between dawn and daylight, shots rang out—and Chivington's troops charged. The soldiers appeared to be coming from all sides. Women, children, and unarmed men were shot down as the troops advanced. With the soldiers almost within touching distance, Indians finally turned to run in terror toward the creek.

The first blast of gunfire killed Left Hand, the Arapaho chief. When Black Kettle saw that he had to run, he called to White Antelope, a Cheyenne chief, to run with him. But 75-year-old White Antelope wrapped his blanket tightly around him, and started to sing his death song. As he solemnly chanted the words, "nothing lives long except the earth and the mountains," a bullet cut him down. Black Kettle was the last to leave.

The attack lasted four hours. Chivington reported between 400 and 500 Indians killed. Most of them were women and children. When all the living had fled and the Indian camp was strewn with bodies, the soldiers looted the tepees and rounded up the mules and horses. They then mutilated the dead, cutting more than a hundred scalps. Weeks later the scalps were exhibited, between the acts, at a theater in Denver.

But Chivington's act did not bring him glory. When the horrors of Sand Creek were made public, protest was loud. Kit Carson, himself a battler of Indians, called it the ac-

tion of "a coward or a dog." Four years after the massacre at Sand Creek, a congressional commission, which included three army generals, said "it scarcely has its parallel in the records of Indian barbarity." The government decided to pay Black Kettle's band—or what remained of it—a large sum of money.

By that time, money and words of regret meant little to the Cheyenne. Black Kettle went south with a handful of followers—still hoping to find peace. The rest of the Southern

Cheyenne began to terrorize the whites. Stage coaches were attacked, their drivers and passengers killed, their cargo and thousands of dollars scattered in the Plains winds. The Indians raided towns, killed cattle, and chopped down telegraph poles.

The Cheyenne trail of looting, burning, and murder moved north. The Indians were heading for the Powder River country, an area west of the Black Hills of South Dakota. Here, where there were plenty of buffalo, were camped the Sioux, the

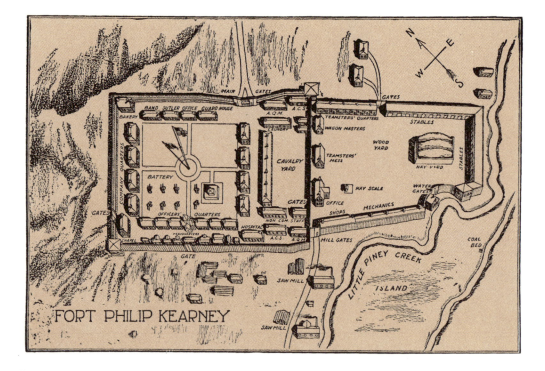

FORT PHILIP KEARNEY

Northern Cheyenne and the Arapaho. The Southern Cheyenne told the story of Sand Creek. Then they offered the war pipe to each chief.

There was no hesitation—the solemn puffs of smoke were a pledge of aid in war against the common enemy. Among the chiefs who smoked the pipe were Red Cloud, Sitting Bull, Man-Afraid-of-His-Horses, Roman Nose, Crazy Horse, Dull Knife —names which were to terrify the Plains in the years to come.

By the spring of 1865, more troops were sent to the western commanders. A plan was laid for a major attack against the Indians in the Powder River country. General Patrick Edward Connor was put in command of three columns. He issued this general order to his troops: "You will not receive overtures of peace and submission from the Indians but will attack and kill every male Indian over twelve years of age." But his men came upon few Indians. Connor destroyed one Cheyenne camp, killing twenty-four, and an Arapaho camp, killing sixty-three. But the campaign proved to be one of the major disasters in United States military history.

Connor was to meet troops under the command of Colonel Nelson Cole and Colonel Samuel Walker on September 1. Then they were to march into the Indian-controlled area. Cole and Walker did not make it. With bad maps and poor guides, the two colonels wandered in circles in the South Dakota Bad Lands.

There was little grass for their horses. The troops ran out of supplies and had to kill their pack mules for food. When some Sioux discovered them they did not have the strength to fight back. A band of Cheyenne under Roman Nose attacked them, but made more of a game of it than a death struggle. By September 8, they still had not reached the Tongue River where they were to rendezvous with Connor.

That day, Connor sent Major Frank North with twenty Pawnee scouts to find the lost troops. North returned three days later to report the remnants of a camp with five or six hundred dead cavalry horses and burnt saddles and bridles lying in the ashes of campfires.

North and his Pawnees went out again, and finally on September 19, the command of 1800 men was found. Not a cavalryman was on a horse. Of the six hundred horses left, not one was strong enough to carry the weight of a man. The men were starving, and pushed toward the Pawnees, begging for hardtack.

Arms had not solved the Indian problem, and in 1865, a commission was sent west to make another peace treaty with the Plains tribes. The Sioux, Cheyenne, and Arapaho were to be given full rights to the Powder River country—a small favor since they were already there in force. In return, the commissioners asked for the right to build forts and roads. Chiefs of a number of small, friendly bands of Indians signed the treaty. But not a single important chief "touched the pen." The next

year, at Fort Laramie, the government proposed still another peace treaty. It could not hurt to listen. Even hostile Chief Red Cloud was present, though he was not ready to sign. E. B. Taylor, the Indian Office representative, told them that the government only wanted to keep open the Bozeman Trail, the best route into the Montana mining area. But he kept back the fact that the treaty demanded new forts and new roads—all through Sioux territory.

Taylor did not even have a chance to make his lie stick. In the midst of the meeting, General Henry B. Carrington came to Fort Laramie with 700 infantrymen. He was to keep the Powder River country safe for white travelers. To do so he would have to build roads and forts. He had made no secret of his plans, but when Red Cloud and his warriors heard them, trouble began. Red Cloud coldly refused to speak to Carrington. He wrapped his blanket tightly around him, sent word to his warriors to break camp, and stalked out of the conference room. With these gestures, he declared war.

Carrington was a brave and conscientious officer. But he knew nothing about Indians or Indian fighting. In July, he set about to build Fort Phil Kearny between two forks of Piney Creek, a branch of the Powder River in Wyoming.

From the first day he set up the temporary tents, he had no peace from the Indians. Soldiers who went

The Wagon Box Fight (above) took place near Fort Phil Kearny, in 1867. Chief Little Wolf, of the Cheyenne (below), burned the fort one year later, after it had been abandoned by the soldiers.

more than a few paces from camp were found dead. Horses were run off, wagon trains were burned. Before the year was out, 150 people were killed in or near the new fort, not in major battles but in minor attacks. But Carrington pushed his men, and the strong wooden fort was completed at the end of October. Carrington also built two other forts on the trail—Fort Reno and Fort C. F. Smith—but they did not offend the Indians as much as Fort Phil Kearny. And it was at Fort Kearny that they gained one of their greatest victories over the whites. Nearly every morning, between ten and eleven, wagons brought wood to the fort from the lumber camp in the nearby hills. The Indians had often harassed the train. Lookouts at the fort were not surprised, on the morning of December 21, 1866, to see signals from a lookout on the hills telling them that Indians were approaching. The wood wagons were under attack.

In the fort, Carrington quickly organized a relief party. He was about to dispatch a small troop under Captain James Powell, when he was approached by William J. Fetterman. Fetterman was a captain who had been cited for bravery in the Civil War, and he begged for the assignment.

Carrington did not want him to have it. Everyone in the fort remembered a recent boast of Fetterman's: "Give me eighty men and I'll ride through the whole Sioux nation." But Fetterman had seniority over Powell, so Carrington gave in. But he made his orders as specific as possible. "Support the wood train, relieve it and report to me," he told Fetterman. "Under no circumstances pursue [the Indians] over Lodge Pole Ridge."

The ridge separated the streams running into the Powder and Tongue Rivers. Fetterman took his

place at the head of his troop—by coincidence, exactly eighty men.

In the next hour, the wood train found itself suddenly free of Indian attackers. It made its way back to the fort in safety. And in that same hour, a small band of Indians came toward Fetterman, taunted his men, and galloped quickly out of reach. Again and again they repeated the action, each time retreating closer and closer to Lodge Pole Ridge. Fet-

Red Cloud, Oglala Sioux chief, and his great-granddaughter, Burning Heart.

Connor was defeated by Roman Nose.

terman disobeyed his orders and began to pursue the Indians.

The decoys had done their job, and from the hills on either side came some two thousand Sioux, Cheyenne, and Arapaho. The fight could not have lasted more than an hour. Fetterman and his entire command were wiped out. Indians counted coup in wholesale numbers.

It was a fight in the old tradition, with bows and arrows, lances and clubs. Hardly any of the Indians had guns. Of the eighty-one men they killed that day, only six showed gun wounds. And there is evidence that Fetterman and one other killed themselves at the last moment. Estimates of Indian losses in the battle vary from fifteen to one hundred and eighty-five.

At Fort Phil Kearny, Carrington heard the firing, and the quiet which followed. He dispatched a rescue party—but it was too late. It could only carry back some of the dead.

The snowstorms which struck Fort Phil Kearny brought a temporary end to Indian attacks. But with the coming of spring, 1867, Indian raids around the fort were stepped up. By midsummer, Red Cloud was ready to repeat the Fetterman victory. It had worked so well before, he saw no need to change his plans of decoy and ambush. In August he got his chance. A detachment of soldiers under Captain Powell, the man whom Fetterman had replaced that tragic day less than seven months earlier, was guarding a wood train. To the Sioux, led by Red Cloud and Crazy Horse, it looked too easy.

Powell's scouts reported Indian movement and he made his plans

Colonel Chivington destroyed Chief Black Kettle's village at Sand Creek.

Captain Fetterman

General Carrington

Jim Beckwourth

carefully. There would be no decoy chasing. He ordered the wagon boxes formed into a circle. Within it, he placed his soldiers and the wood-cutters. There were twenty-eight soldiers and four civilians; most of the woodcutters had fled to the fort. Powell issued arms and ammunition. But now, the rifles were brand new breech-loading rifles.

The Indians changed their strategy and attacked with shouts of joy. The younger men and those on the faster horses rode in as swiftly as possible to be able to count the first coups. They were met by a blast of fire, but they were used to this. Now, as always, while the white soldiers paused to reload, the Indians would sweep forward to victory.

But the white soldiers did not have to reload. Immediately after the first round of firing there came another, then another, and another. The brave Sioux warriors fell back, regrouped, charged again. Throughout the morning the battle followed the same pattern. And then, with nearly 200 of his warriors lying dead or wounded on the battlefield, Red Cloud gave up. Powell had three dead and two wounded.

The Wagon Box battle was revenge for the Fetterman disaster. But it did not change the fate of Fort Phil Kearny. In April, 1868, a new peace commission met with Indian chiefs at Fort Laramie and agreed to give up its forts and roads in the Powder River country. This time, Red Cloud and some other chiefs regarded as hostile signed the treaty—although not until after the forts were actually abandoned. That summer, the flag at Fort Phil Kearny was struck, and the troops marched solemnly out.

Before they were completely out of sight of the wooden palisades, a band of hostile Indians entered the fort and set torches to the walls and buildings. The smoke spiraled upward and then hung in the still August air, mocking the retreating soldiers.

The coming of the railroad threatened not only the Indians, but also the buffalo they lived upon. Soon after railroads were built through the Plains, and before farmers had come West to till the soil, there was little freight to ship back East except for buffalo hides and bones. The Santa Fe Railroad is said to have shipped nearly six million buffalo hides from Kansas. And in 1873 and 1874, 8,000 tons of bones per year were shipped for bone china. Piles of bones and hides awaiting removal are pictured above.

"Buffalo Bill" Cody was fourteen when he went West in 1860. After serving as a scout, he earned his nickname killing buffalo to feed construction workers on the Kansas Pacific RR.

THE IRON HORSE
AND THE
WHISPERING WIRES

The Plains Indians called the railroad the Iron Horse or the Iron Snake, and they called the telegraph the Talking or Whispering Wires. As each poked its way west it chipped away at the Indian's freedom.

When the first transcontinental railroad was completed just west of Ogden, Utah, in 1869, it meant that the hazardous days of travel on the old Oregon and Santa Fe trails were over.

"Union Pacific Railroad," a rare old lithograph, shows groups of Plains Indians hiding in the shadows, and tearing up ties and rails to cause a train wreck. Attacks on the Union Pacific were frequent during the summer and fall of 1867, as the iron rails moved into the Black Hills of Wyoming.

Trains also played their part in wiping out the vast buffalo herds. In 1872 and 1873 alone, freight cars traveling back East from Kansas were loaded with 1,250,000 hides. Of the more than 50,000,000 buffalo on the Plains in 1850, almost all had disappeared by 1885. Slaughtering the buffalo, as General Phil Sheridan pointed out, amounted to destroying the "Indians' commissary."

The telegraph, which crossed the continent late in 1861, was immediately put to use by the army whenever Indian trouble flared up. The Indians understood this well, and telegraph stations and lines were high on their list of objects marked for destruction.

When the telegraph was built through Utah, it followed the route of the Union Pacific.

Handbook to the Gold Fields *(below)* may even have been used by *"forty-niners"* *(right)* in California, for gold continued to be found there in quantity up until as late as 1860.

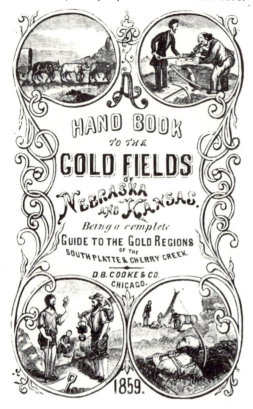

PROSPECTING FOR GOLD

The discovery of gold in California in 1848 sent droves of gold-seeking "forty-niners" across the Plains in the following year. Ten years later, when gold was discovered in Colorado in 1858, "Pike's Peak or Bust" became the rallying cry of thousands of prospectors—rough, hardy men willing to brave the dangers of drought and Indian attack for a chance to "strike paydirt."

In 1858, 25,000 miners passed through Fort Leavenworth, Kansas, on their way to the gold fields in Pike's Peak, Colorado. The canvas tops of their wagons were often lettered "Pike's Peak or Bust!"

The mining camp called Deadwood City grew up overnight in the Black Hills of South Dakota after gold was found there in 1875. In its early days it was the home of Calamity Jane, and frontier marshal Wild Bill Hickok.

The goldrush into the Black Hills of South Dakota and Wyoming in 1874 brought the hated whites into Pa Sapa—the sacred territory of the Sioux. Here the Indians would make a stand. The 6,000 square miles of land had been guaranteed them by Federal treaty. But neither the army nor the Indians could stop the rush of hordes of men who "would rather be scalped than poor."

The white invasion of the Black Hills was not the only reason for the Sioux War of 1876, but coming as it did on top of rushes into Colorado and Montana, it was an important factor. So the gold seekers, too, played their part in a greater drama, for the Sioux War led to the final defeat of the Plains Indians.

This old daguerreotype made fun of gold-hunters and the equipment they carried.

113

Chief Roman Nose, of the Cheyenne.

And there was the white man himself. The Indians could understand and respect the soldiers. They were doing their job, and doing it well. When they fought, they were brave and intelligent foes. But those who did not fight were more difficult to understand—the commissioners who talked peace, the agents who lied and cheated, and the gold-seekers. The white man's speech was often crooked. Time and again he put his pen to paper promising freedom to the Indian. And too often his promise was broken.

ON THE WARPATH

The world of sun and sky and buffalo, which the Indian knew so well, was changing. Strange things were breaking the long line of the horizon: the telegraph pole, the railroad. Homesteaders, ranchers, and longhorn cattle appeared. And familiar things were passing away. The buffalo had begun to disappear. Now there were Indians who were happy to take the white man's handouts and live peaceably on reservations. Now there were more Indian scouts than ever before, eager to serve the white man's soldiers.

United States Cavalrymen here take cover behind their dead horses, just as they had to do during the Beecher Island Fight.

114

The eight years between Fort Phil Kearny and the Battle of Little Big Horn were years of broken promises. Many Indians saw that their old way of life was passing, and tried to travel the white man's path in peace. But during those eight years, other tribes fought desperately to preserve their lands and their traditions.

Roman Nose

Among the Northern Cheyenne one fighter became especially famous. He was Roman Nose, a handsome brave who stood six feet three inches tall and weighed 230 pounds.

His battle skill was so great that many of his own tribe thought him completely bulletproof.

But Roman Nose was to die in battle, bravely, in a skirmish with white soldiers which U.S. military histories call the Beecher Island Fight. It took place on September 17, 1868. The leader of the white force was Major George A. Forsyth. His command was not made up of military men, but of frontiersmen who had volunteered to seek out and fight Indians. They were well armed—with repeating rifles and Colt re-

General Crook

General Sherman

Major Forsyth

Lt. Col. Cus

volvers—as they reached the Arickaree Fork of the Republican River and sighted Indians.

Forsyth ordered a halt and proceeded to make camp on a small island in the stream to withstand the expected attack. Nearby were camps of Sioux, Cheyenne, and Arapaho, among them Roman Nose and his band. The Indians attacked at dawn. Forsyth's losses were heavy, but he held off the enemy.

By noon, Roman Nose had not yet taken part, and his Cheyenne warriors, although fighting bravely, were downcast. They believed so firmly in Roman Nose and his medicine that they could fight their hardest only when he led them.

Some of his followers rode back to talk to him. Roman Nose had never before needed to be urged into battle. Then the explanation came, haltingly and grimly. Roman Nose's

Roman Nose's Cheyenne warriors attacking Major Forsyth's troops at Beecher Island.

war medicine forbade him to eat food removed from a pot or pan with an iron implement. But the day before, without his knowing it at the time, the bread he had eaten had been handled by an iron utensil. "If I go into this fight," he told his companions, "I shall be killed."

On the battlefield, Indians were dying, cut down by repeating rifles and Colts. Roman Nose looked about and saw his men lying dead and wounded. Without a further word, he took out his package of war paint, daubed himself, took his war bonnet out of its sacred packet, put it on, and mounted his favorite war pony. In his heart he knew that this was the day of his death—but he rode strongly and bravely toward the white force on Beecher Island. Behind him, his braves followed; their leader was in action. Roman Nose pushed his horse faster and faster—and rode directly into the soldiers. They missed him as he came forward, but as he passed them, a bullet caught him in the back. Still he rode, and did not fall off his horse until he reached the other bank of the river.

Roman Nose was carried back to the Cheyenne camp and died that afternoon. His warriors continued their charges against the whites, but they were weak attacks. Roman Nose and his good medicine were no longer theirs. The Battle of Beecher Island belonged to the whites.

Black Kettle

Despite the treachery he had met with at Sand Creek, Chief Black Kettle continued to urge his band of Cheyenne to have peaceful dealings with the white men.

After Sand Creek, Black Kettle had led his people into Indian Territory—the present state of Oklahoma. In the fall of 1868 they

Custer's cavalry charge on Black Kettle's Washita River encampment, in Oklahoma.

camped on the Washita River. He rode into Fort Cobb to seek permission to move his camp nearer the fort. Colonel W. B. Hazen, commander of the fort, had no authority to deal with friendly Indians. General Sheridan had made it quite clear that there were no such Indians as friendly Indians.

Black Kettle went back to his camp. He did not know it then, but two Cheyenne war parties had just arrived on the Washita, fresh from raids in Kansas. Bear Shield and Crow Neck, their leaders, were planning a scalp dance to celebrate.

But it was Black Kettle's band that was to pay for the Cheyenne crimes, hunted down by Lt. Colonel George Armstrong Custer—a hero of the Civil War. Custer had been assigned to help clean up the Indian raiders on the southern Plains. On the night of November 26, with snow whirling about, his scouts reported an unidentified Cheyenne camp ahead. The next morning Custer attacked.

As the bugler sounded "Garry Owen," the Seventh Cavalry's lively call to attack, Custer's men swooped down on Black Kettle's village. Amid the screams of the women and children and the surprised shouts of the men, Custer's cavalry kept up a steady fire. A few Cheyenne managed to reach weapons and fight back. But most of them were killed in front of their tepees. Black Kettle and his wife died together in the first terrible assault.

Kiowa chiefs: Lone Wolf (above) and Satanta. The Kiowa lived in the Texas Panhandle, but raided deep into Mexico.

More than one hundred Cheyenne were killed; more than fifty women and children captured. Custer had destroyed 700 horses, 4,000 arrows, 1,000 buffalo robes, 1,000 pounds of lead and 500 pounds of powder. But he had also destroyed Black Kettle, the man who wanted peace.

Satanta

On the southern Plains no more warlike tribe existed than the Kiowa. And of all the Kiowa chiefs none was more warlike than White Bear, sometimes known as Satanta. Until his death, Satanta never ceased fighting the white invaders of Kiowa territory.

Soon after Custer's attack on the Washita, Satanta and Lone Wolf, another Kiowa chief, voluntarily offered to surrender. Winter was coming on, and life on a reservation, which guaranteed food and warmth, was welcome during cold weather. The chiefs knew that they could return to warfare, if they chose, when spring came once again.

And in the spring of 1871, Satanta and a number of followers did leave the white man's reservation. In Texas they found their quarry— a wagon train. In no time at all they killed its seven occupants, and returned to the reservation. Unfortunately for Satanta and his lieutenants, General William T. Sherman was present. He had come west to see for himself how the campaigns against the Indians were proceeding. Satanta was no coward. He walked cheerfully forward to meet the general. Satanta admitted the raid in Texas, even naming the In-

Custer's Seventh Cavalry destroying Black Kettle's village on the Washita.

dians who had taken part in it with him. Sherman ordered the arrest of the three major Kiowa chiefs: Satanta, Satank, and Big Tree, and sent them to Texas for trial.

Only Satanta and Big Tree made it to Texas, for Satank was shot when he attacked his guards.

A Texas court sentenced Satanta and Big Tree to death. But Indian agents thought that their hanging would set off a dangerous uprising. Instead they saw to it that the sentence was changed to life imprisonment. Even that was too much for Satanta's friends. The Kiowa, joined by the Cheyenne, threatened to strike if Satanta and Big Tree were not freed. The threat of raids —and actual raids—continued until October, 1873, when the two men were released. Immediately they rode off to lead new raids.

Big Tree was never recaptured, but Satanta was arrested soon after, and sent to prison at Huntsville, Texas. In the fall of 1876, after spending two years in his cell, he announced that he was ill. Guards brought him to the prison hospital. There, Satanta went to a window, two stories from the ground. He sang his death song, and jumped to the courtyard. He was dead before anyone could reach him.

Chief Big Tree (above) and Chief Satank (below) led Kiowa uprisings in Texas.

Sitting Bull

In the Powder River country, west of the Black Hills, in southeastern Montana, the Sioux had managed to live free and undisturbed since the Bozeman Trail and the forts in their area had been abandoned. There had been some whites in the territory, of course, and there were always rumors that the Northern Pacific Railroad would be continued beyond its terminal point at Bismarck, North Dakota.

But until the summer of 1874, the Sioux—joined by the Cheyenne and the Arapaho—enjoyed more freedom than most Plains Indians. And the fiercest leader of the hostile Indians was Sitting Bull, chief of the Hunkpapa band of the Sioux. He vowed never to live on a reservation.

In 1874, Sitting Bull and Crazy Horse, chief of the Oglala Sioux, saw unmistakable signs of their freedom's end. That summer, the treaty which promised the Sioux sole use of the Black Hills and the Powder River country, was violated when Custer led the Seventh Cavalry into the Black Hills.

He announced that the purpose of the trip was to test the soil, and to determine its gold content. Rumors of gold in the Black Hills had been current for months. The Sioux made no effort to halt Custer's party. They referred to the trail of his expedition as "the thieves road."

Custer reported "gold in the grassroots." The country was then in the grip of a depression, and his words set off a rush not seen since the discovery of gold in Colorado, in 1858.

Since the government found it impossible to keep prospectors out of the Black Hills, it offered to buy the land from the Indians, so that war might be avoided. But the hostile chiefs purposely put such a high price on their property that the plan could not succeed.

From Sitting Bull's camp on the Powder River, the word spread: there would be fighting as soon as winter was over.

In December, 1875, the Secretary of the Interior flatly ordered all Indians to move to reservations by January 31, 1876, or be "deemed hostile and treated accordingly by the military force." If word got to Sitting Bull and Crazy Horse in time (which is doubtful), they chose to ignore it.

In March, Colonel J. J. Reynolds of the Third Cavalry attacked a village on the Powder River. He surprised the Indians but he did not follow up his advantage. As a result, the warriors saw the women and children to safety and returned to fight Reynolds. He was forced to retreat, leaving his dead and wounded to the Indians—disgraceful conduct by army standards.

The victory over Reynolds raised the morale of the hostiles. By June, nearly 1,000 of the best fighting men among the Sioux and Cheyenne were gathered under the leadership of Sitting Bull.

The first fighting took place with General George Crook at the Rosebud River. There were very few casualties on either side, but Crook was badly beaten and the Indians remained in control of their land. It was another boost to their morale, and another reason for more Indian fighters to join Sitting Bull.

After the Rosebud battle, the successful Indians moved their camp. It was so large that the Indians believed their new position could never be kept secret. They had moved to the banks of the Little Big Horn River, which was to become the most famous battleground in Plains Indian history.

CUSTER'S
LAST STAND

On the banks of the Rosebud, a few days before the battle with Crook, Sitting Bull had participated in a Sun Dance. At dawn, he placed himself with his back to the sacred pole. He watched, without change of expression, while a tribesman dug tiny bits of skin out of his arm and cut them off with a knife.

Fifty times he was cut on the right arm, the man with the awl working from the wrist to the shoulder, and fifty times on the left arm. Then, streaming blood, Sitting Bull rose to dance. He faced the sun from

Chief Gall, a Hunkpapa Teton Sioux, helped win the Battle of Little Big Horn.

the time of its rising to the time of its setting. Then, as he so desperately hoped to do, he fell into a trance.

Sitting Bull's vision in that trance was a good one: soldiers and Indians on horseback falling upside down into his camp. Eight days after the Battle of the Rosebud, Sitting Bull's vision was to become reality.

On the night of June 24, 1876, Arikara and Crow scouts for the United States Seventh Cavalry reported to their commanding officer, Lt. Colonel George Armstrong Custer. They told him they had found an Indian trail. Custer too, had had a vision, which he confided to the scouts: he would gain a victory over the Indians on this battlefield—a victory that would lead to his becoming President of the United

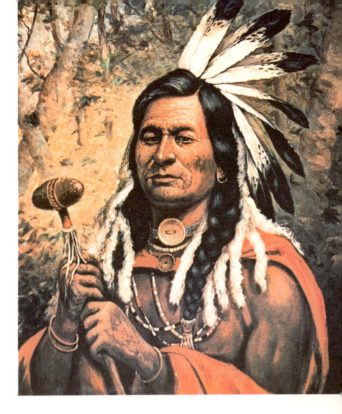

The noted Sioux, Chief Rain-in-the-Face, was present at the Fetterman massacre.

States. To attain his victory Custer would rely on the strategy that had been so successful against Black Kettle at Washita. He would divide his forces and attack from two sides at once. He knew he had to move fast because there were reports that his troops had been seen. The Indian camp on the Little Big Horn would surely expect an attack, and the tribes would be prepared.

Three troops of cavalry under Major Marcus A. Reno were sent across the river, above the village the scouts had reported. Three troops under Captain Frederick W. Benteen were to head for the village from the southwest. One troop was put in charge of the pack train and ordered to follow Reno. Custer himself (or "Long Hair," as the Indians called him) was to lead five troops across the river, to attack from the east. Benteen seems to have been thoroughly confused by his orders, but Reno jogged ahead and was the first to arrive at Sitting Bull's camp. As always when thus surprised, the Indian camp was thrown into complete confusion. But this time the Indians recovered quickly.

Sitting Bull leaped out of his tepee and shouted encouragement as his braves mounted their war

Chief Red Horn Bull, an Oglala Sioux, was wounded leading the attack on Reno.

ponies to battle with the cavalrymen. Then Reno made a mistake. He ordered his troops to dismount and fight on the ground. The men, still not certain how many Indians they faced, dismounted and took up a position among some trees on the river

bank. As far as Reno knew, Custer would be along any minute.

There were bluffs across the river. They seemed to be the logical place to go if Custer did not appear soon. Minutes passed and there was no sign of Custer's troops. When a bullet smashed into the face of Bloody Knife, the scout standing beside him, Reno made his decision. He shouted orders for the men to mount their horses and to retreat across the river.

Not all the troopers heard the orders. But once Reno and those nearest him turned into the river, the rout began. Joyous Indians sent arrows and bullets after Reno's men—

and even rode up close enough to use their lances and clubs.

Although Reno's men were not given much chance to fight, they were brave in retreat. Many stopped to help the wounded, and to pick up those whose horses had been killed. It took three or four minutes to cross the Little Big Horn, but there was trouble on the other side; the bluff above the bank was eight feet high.

As the men scrambled up, leading their horses, the Indians kept firing steadily across the river. By the time Reno's command made it to the bluffs, the Indians on the opposite bank seemed to fade from sight. The firing ceased except for a few parting shots as the Indians moved down river. Reno and his men were certain that the Indian movement meant that Custer was attacking. At that precise moment, Benteen's battalion came into view.

His fresh troops met what was left of Reno's force. Thirty-two officers and men were dead, ten wounded and nineteen were missing—one-third of his battalion. Neither Reno nor Benteen followed in the direction toward which the Indians were moving. But by now they heard shooting, which could only mean that Custer was in battle.

Custer had watched Reno and Benteen and their troops march off

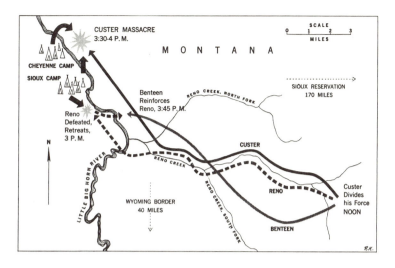

Major Reno (above) was ordered to attack separately. Map traces moves of Custer, Reno, and Benteen.

as ordered, and had then proceeded with his five companies to the lower end of the Indian camp.

It seems likely that he expected Reno to engage the Indians long enough for him to attack from the rear with his own troops, thus bringing a pincers together for what should have been an easy victory. But Custer did not know, as he rode off, that the brush on the opposite bank of the river hid more than 3,000 Sioux and Cheyenne.

Custer led his men across a ravine opposite a Sioux encampment at a ford in the Little Big Horn. The

Major Reno's troops retreat from the Sioux camp, toward the Little Big Horn River.

sight of their many tepees must have been his first indication that this was no small Indian gathering.

But by this time he had committed himself, and he knew that Reno had already started his attack. In fact, from a ridge, he probably could see Reno leading his men. He quite naturally expected the Indians to scatter under Reno's charge.

Custer was a brave soldier, and often a foolhardy one. Today he was taking his largest risk, but he was also wise enough to seek help. He ordered W. W. Cooke, his adjutant, to get a message to Benteen. The excited message was quickly scrawled on a piece of note paper: "Benteen—come on—big village—be quick—bring packs. P.S. Bring packs."

after receiving the message, Benteen came upon Reno's retreating men. By that time Custer was engaged.

Trumpeter Martin was the last white man to see Custer alive and tell about it. From the moment Martin left with the message for Benteen, all of what followed for Custer and his soldiers is in doubt.

Only the Indians could have told what really happened.

It is likely that Custer led his men down the slopes leading to the bank of the Little Big Horn opposite the camp he had sighted. Indians who were there confirm this, although there are differing accounts as to how far the cavalrymen rode. Some say they went as far as the river bank, others say they stopped a half mile short of it. But it is generally agreed that Custer did not cross the river. He had been seen by the Indians as he came down the ravine, and from then on there was no way of stopping the battle.

Custer's position had been reported to Sitting Bull and Crazy Horse. They wheeled from the fleeing Reno and turned toward the fresh target. They attacked "Long Hair's" troops from the rear so swiftly and in such numbers that many of the soldiers did not have a chance to dismount

The trumpeter, a young Italian immigrant named Martin, was dispatched with the message, and Custer turned once more to survey the scene ahead. Martin delivered the message, although his horse was wounded by a stray bullet from Reno's battle. Benteen chose to ignore Custer's order for reasons which have never been made clear. Soon

127

Sitting Bull's Winchester rifle, taken from him when he surrendered in 1881.

and fight, but died in their saddles. Ahead of Custer, other Indians were also attacking. Then, Indians appeared on the sides as well. They formed a complete circle of death.

Fighting gallantly, what was now left of Custer's command—two companies and remnants of a third—moved toward the ridge on the other side of a deep gulch. The top of the hill must have seemed safer than low ground. They never made it. Coming over the other side of the ridge was Crazy Horse and his band of warriors. And along this ridge Custer made his famous last stand.

It was not an ideal spot for defense, but with Indians pressing in, there was no choice. Nobody knows how many cavalrymen were left at this time; the guesses range from forty to a hundred. The men must have known they could not survive this battle, but they were prepared to kill as many Indians as possible before it ended. Some shot their horses and dragged the bodies to form a circle of cover. Some turned their horses loose, perhaps in the wild hope that they would confuse the Indians.

Wave after wave of Indians—some with guns, most with bows and arrows, many with clubs—swooped by the besieged men. In the excitement many an Indian was knocked from his horse by another Indian; a few were later found dead with arrows in them.

Nothing could have changed the outcome. One by one the soldiers were picked off. Then, when only a few were left, the Indians made one last charge and finished them off with clubs. The whole battle, from the time Custer rode down the ra-

Sitting Bull's nephew, Chief White Bull, (left) claimed he had counted coup on, and killed Custer. White Bull drew a picture of the event (right) but nobody knows positively who Custer's killer was.

This sketch of Plains Indians on the warpath appeared in 1870 in Harper's Weekly.

Colt .44 Army revolver used by General George Custer in the Civil War.

vine to the moment the last bullet was fired from the ridge, could not have lasted more than an hour. More than 200 cavalrymen lay dead. The only survivor of Custer's command was a horse named Comanche.

With just a short pause for stripping the bodies and gathering guns and other valuables, the Sioux and Cheyenne regrouped. To the south were more white soldiers: the defeated troops of Major Reno and the recently arrived men of Captain Benteen. With wild shouts the Indians rushed to new battle.

Neither Reno nor Benteen were yet aware of Custer's disaster. They had spent the afternoon trying to establish themselves in the best pos-

sible defensive position. But they
had not chosen well. In the three
daylight hours left that day, the
Indians killed eighteen and wounded
forty-six more cavalrymen.

The Indians did not keep up their
attack after dark, but it was not a
peaceful night for the soldiers.
There were the wounded to care for
and defenses to build—with the few

axes and shovels which remained,
and with tin cups and bare hands.

But nothing could change the fact
that the troops were in a poor position, surrounded by ravines behind
which Indians could hide and ridges
from which they could fire in almost
complete safety. The desperate situ-
ation was not helped by their lack
of knowledge of what had happened

warned against attacking the surrounded soldiers.

Another version tells how Sitting Bull himself called off the attack because he was afraid that killing so many soldiers in one day would guarantee the sending of even larger armies against the Indians. Whatever the reason, the Reno-Benteen forces escaped disaster.

The next day the troops of Brigadier General Alfred H. Terry and Colonel John Gibbon found the Reno-Benteen troops—and told them of Custer's defeat. Then began the dismal job of identifying—and burying—the dead.

Among the many unanswered questions raised on this black day for the United States Cavalry, two especially have troubled historians. Was Custer the last man to die? Who killed him?

There are, of course, no reliable answers. According to Indian testimony, Custer was killed early in the battle. He was not, as some paintings of the battle show him, the last man standing, saber in one hand, gun in another, fighting off Indians. In fact, the Seventh Cavalry never took sabers into Indian battle.

It is possible that he was killed in the first Indian assault, but no one will ever know for sure. Nor for

to Custer. An attempt was made to send scouts through. It failed. Reno was surrounded by Indians.

Daybreak of June 26 came early—about 3 A.M.—and the Indians attacked again. But they did not come in full force. No one seems to know why. By nightfall the Indians had faded from sight. One Indian chief later said that some medicine men

that matter are we ever likely to know who actually killed Custer.

Henry Wadsworth Longfellow wrote a poem called "The Revenge of Rain-in-the-Face" in which he identified that chief as the killer. Rain-in-the-Face himself sometimes said yes and sometimes no. .The Cheyenne have claimed the credit for one of their own; and the Sioux have had their candidates.

The most recent claim has been made for White Bull, a Sioux chief, who was twenty-six years old at the time of the battle. He told his story in 1932, fifty-six years after it took place, and there were other old Indians who verified it. It is not likely that White Bull's version will end the mystery. There will always be mystery whenever Custer's Last Stand is discussed.

The mysteries did not begin to accumulate until much later. All America was shocked by Custer's defeat. The news came on a great national holiday—the hundredth anniversary of American Independence, the Fourth of July, 1876.

Not since Abraham Lincoln's death had the country experienced such deep sorrow. Custer, the Civil War hero; Custer, the gallant commander, had suffered failure and death. It was a defeat for the entire United States.

Yet, in the end, it was the Plains Indians who lost at the Little Big Horn. The shock of Custer's defeat aroused the entire United States. People demanded that the government end the Indian threat forever.

As for the Indians, not even Sitting Bull could keep together a force as large as that which fought Custer. There was not enough food in a single area to feed that many. Soon, many who had come from reservations to join the battle, returned to them. The hostiles wandered off in bands to find new hunting grounds.

Sitting Bull became the main target of the white soldiers in the Yellowstone area. The troops were commanded by General Nelson A. Miles, who had put down the

Dull Knife and his Cheyenne warriors were present at the Custer massacre.

132

southern Plains tribes two years earlier. Miles wanted to bring Sitting Bull to a reservation. But after two meetings, Miles knew Sitting Bull would not come of his own free will. Sitting Bull had said: "God Almighty make me an Indian—and not an agency Indian."

Miles had no choice. He chased Sitting Bull. They never came face to face in battle—but Sitting Bull was forced to cross the American border into Canada.

The world he knew was ending. Red Cloud had long since led his band onto the reservation. Crazy Horse, pursued by Miles, surrendered at the Red Cloud Agency. (In September, 1877, the great chief of the Oglala Sioux died resisting arrest.) Dull Knife, chief of the Northern Cheyenne, also surrendered.

And finally, with no buffalo to hunt in Canada, Sitting Bull led his band south, and on July 18, 1881, he surrendered at Fort Buford, North Dakota. In 1883, he was moved to the Standing Rock Agency.

Here and there throughout the Plains there were occasional Indian raids and some killings. But the United States now had plenty of experienced Indian fighters in the field. That, and the disappearance of the buffalo from the Plains, brought the last of the Indians to the reservations.

The "bloody battle" was headlined in the New York Herald *on July 6, 1876.*

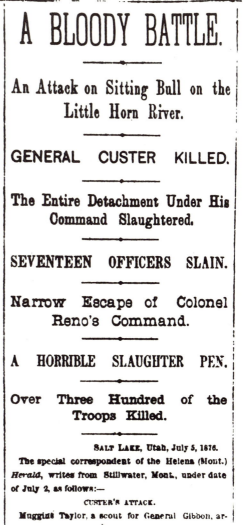

A BLOODY BATTLE.

An Attack on Sitting Bull on the Little Horn River.

GENERAL CUSTER KILLED.

The Entire Detachment Under His Command Slaughtered.

SEVENTEEN OFFICERS SLAIN.

Narrow Escape of Colonel Reno's Command.

A HORRIBLE SLAUGHTER PEN.

Over Three Hundred of the Troops Killed.

SALT LAKE, Utah, July 5, 1876.

The special correspondent of the Helena (Mont.) *Herald*, writes from Stillwater, Mont., under date of July 2, as follows:—

CUSTER'S ATTACK.

Muggins Taylor, a scout for General Gibbon, arrived here last night direct from Little Horn River, and reports that General Custer found the Indian camp of 2,000 lodges on the Little Horn and immediately attacked it.

TRACED BY THE DEAD.

He charged the thickest portion of the camp with five companies. Nothing is known of the operations of this detachment except their course as traced by the dead.

MAJOR RENO'S ATTACK.

Major Reno commanded the other seven companies and attacked the lower portion of the camp.

CUSTER KILLED.

The Indians poured a murderous fire from all directions. General Custer, his two brothers, his nephew and brother-in-law were all killed, and not one of his detachment escaped.

THREE HUNDRED KILLED.

Two hundred and seven men were buried in one place. The number of killed is estimated at 300 and the wounded at 31.

FOUGHT LIKE TIGERS.

The Indians surrounded Major Reno's command and held them one day in the hills, cut off from water, until Gibbon's command came in sight, when they broke camp in the night and left. The Seventh fought like tigers and were overcome by mere brute

Arapaho men and women chant and circle as they perform the Ghost Dance.

THE LAST GHOST

In much of California and Nevada, the year 1889 began with a total eclipse of the sun. That New Year's Day, near Walker Lake, at the southwestern corner of Nevada, a 34-year-old Paiute Indian named Wovoka lay ill. During the brief moments when the moon blotted out the light of the sun over Wovoka's head, he went into a trance.

In his trance, as he told it later, Wovoka died, and his soul was carried to heaven. There, he said, he saw God, surrounded by "all the people who had died long ago engaged in their old time sports and occupations, all happy and forever young."

But Wovoka was not yet ready to enjoy this happy place. God commanded him to return to earth to tell the living that "they must be good and love one another, have no quarreling, and live in peace with the whites; that they must put away all the old practices that savored of war; that if they faithfully obeyed his instructions, they would at last be reunited with their friends in the other world." With the command, a dance was described to Wovoka which he was to teach the Indians. As he came out of his trance, Wovoka knew he was reborn.

Within months, Wovoka's teachings spread from Walker Lake to the Plains. Wovoka himself was received as the man who would lead the Indians from misery to eternal joy—to a heaven without white tormentors. As they waited the coming of their leader, the Indians danced the Ghost Dance, the expression of their new belief.

Nobody really knows why Wovoka's words proved to be so powerful. It may have been that his vision came at a time when it was desperately needed. Disease had killed many Plains Indians. They hated living on the reservations. The buffalo had disappeared. Drought had ruined the crops.

So Wovoka and his teachings were welcomed by many tribes, some more than 2,000 miles away from Walker Lake, Nevada. Pilgrimages to his village were organized. A Cheyenne who was among the first to visit Walker Lake said that representatives of fifteen or sixteen tribes were present at the same time. Wovoka especially attracted the Plains Indians.

Like the Sun Dance before it, which the whites had suppressed, the Ghost Dance was a test of physical strength. Many dancers died from going without food and water during the five day ritual. As many as 400 to 500 Indians would take part in a Ghost Dance. Often the

By 1885, nearly all the buffalo had been slaughtered for hides. Their disappearance meant misery for the Plains Indians, who had depended on them for food.

dance area would be blocked by those who fell, happy and exhausted, to the ground. For this was the object: to attain a trance in which there would come a vision—of dead relatives, of herds of buffalo, of brave deeds in warfare, or of any reminder of the happy past.

But the Ghost Dance, which Wovoka had started in the spirit of peace, was to end in blood. The Sioux, Arapaho, Cheyenne, and Ki-

Plains Indians chewed bits of the cactus (left) called peyote. It contains a substance which brings on bright visions and a sense of well-being. Peyote was most popular in the era of the Ghost Dance — during a time of sorrow and despair for the Indians.

owa Apaches changed the Ghost Dance from the symbol of brotherly love and peace to one of revenge and victory over the white soldiers.

Within a year after Wovoka saw his vision, wild stories and reports were spreading among whites throughout the West. Soon, they began to appear in Eastern newspapers under frightening headlines. The Indians, they said, were about to go on the warpath.

As was usual in those days, Sitting Bull was blamed for the Ghost Dance. Yet as far as any one knows, Sitting Bull had not accepted it as eagerly as some of the other chiefs had, and he was certainly not making any war plans at the time. White settlers left their homes in the country looking for safety in towns and cities. In the fall of 1890, frightened Indian agents called for more troops in South Dakota. As the soldiers moved in, more than 2,000 Sioux moved their tepees—and the Ghost Dance—to the Dakota Badlands. South Dakota, soon after celebrating its first anniversary as a state of the union, prepared for trouble.

General Nelson A. Miles, who had fought Sitting Bull and captured Crazy Horse, now took command. Throughout his Indian fighting career, General Miles had always avoided battle if he could get the Indians to surrender peaceably. He decided to arrest Sitting Bull.

An Arapaho Ghost Shirt. Worn during the Ghost Dance, the shirt might also be worn in battle. The Sioux believed designs protected wearers from bullets of the white man.

Early in December, Sitting Bull was told that Wovoka was coming to aid the Sioux because the whites planned war. Sitting Bull decided this was the time to visit Pine Ridge in the southern part of the state, and asked for a pass. Major William McLaughlin, head of the Standing Rock Agency, was sure the trip would set off an uprising.

At once, without waiting for Miles' approval, he ordered his men to arrest Sitting Bull. On the morning of December 15, a detachment of thirty-three Indian police—Indians employed by the Bureau of Indian Affairs—were sent in.

They marched to the chief's cabin. It was early. Sitting Bull was not yet awake. As the leader of the Indian police prodded him and told him to put his clothes on, his anger burst.

A peyote ceremony. Plains Indians sometimes spent entire nights taking peyote, shaking rattles, and singing songs, waiting for visions to appear.

Colonel Forsyth

General Miles

Chief Sitting Bull

Within minutes, his cabin was surrounded by his warriors. But they were helpless in the face of so many armed men. Amid the cries and shouts of the men and the wail of the women, there suddenly came Sitting Bull's voice. "I am not going," he said. Then the Indian police began firing.

One bullet went through Sitting Bull's body, another into his back. Within seconds he was dead. Next the police ran from their fallen victim and returned to Sitting Bull's cabin. There they killed Crow Foot, Sitting Bull's seventeen-year-old son.

Sitting Bull's death broke the spirit of the Sioux. Although there was some scattered fighting, most of the Sioux started to move back to the agencies. The rest of Sitting Bull's villagers joined Chief Big Foot on the Cheyenne River, in the Bad Lands north of the Pine Ridge Agency, hoping to find some way to get revenge.

Orders were next given to arrest Big Foot. The chief and his loyal followers were surrounded by 3,000 men. Big Foot, ill with pneumonia, surrendered without a shot being fired. On December 28, he and 250 men, women, and children were brought to the army encampment near Wounded Knee Creek, a few miles northeast of Pine Ridge. The next day, Colonel J. W. Forsyth, commander of the Seventh Cavalry, set 500 men around the Indians and ordered them to give up their arms.

Perhaps the Sioux did not quite understand the orders. Perhaps they were simply disobedient. At any rate, their guns and rifles were slow to come forth.

Forsyth decided to speed things up. He sent his men into the tepees in squad formation. The soldiers marched forward, as sullen, frightened women and children scattered before them. The camp's furniture was overturned. Clothes were scattered as the soldiers looked for hidden weapons. At this point, Yellow Bird, a medicine man, shouted to the braves that their shirts were bul-

General Miles and Sitting Bull, at a peace council, soon after Custer's defeat.

letproof. They should attack the invaders. And as a soldier grabbed a blanket, Yellow Bird threw some dirt. As if this gesture were a signal, someone fired a rifle.

The Seventh Cavalry started firing their deadly Hotchkiss repeating guns. In the first volley, nearly half of Big Foot's men were killed or wounded. Indians who escaped the shots turned and ran, with the soldiers after them, firing as they went. Bodies of women and children were found three miles away. By nine at night the massacre was over.

Later, General Miles reported that more than 200 Indians were killed at Wounded Knee—sixty-two of them women and children. The Indians had managed to kill twenty-nine whites and to wound thirty-three. But the Seventh had avenged Little Big Horn.

General Miles was enraged by the massacre. He charged Forsyth with misconduct, but nothing ever came of it. Forsyth was cleared by the Secretary of War.

With 8,000 troops at his command, General Miles slowly forced the remaining Sioux to yield. By January 15, nearly all of them were on reservations. Some stragglers still managed to remain outside—but none of them would ever perform a Ghost Dance again.

CATTLE AND BARBED WIRE

Even before the Civil War, the plains of Texas began filling with long-horned cattle brought north from Mexico. These herds were descended from the cattle brought to America by Spaniards in the 1600's. By the end of the war, there were 6,000,000 cattle in Texas, and home-coming war veterans soon saw that fortunes could be made in ranching, as there was a fine market for beef in the growing cities of the East.

And so the cowboy appeared on the southern Plains. His life on the range made him tough and independent.

But his free life on the open range lasted only a brief period, for homesteaders who planned to farm the land, or to raise sheep, began fencing off their lands with an invention which appeared in 1873—barbed wire.

The arrival of farmers and fence builders, the killing of the buffalo, and the retreat of the Indian to the reservation meant that the wild, free days of the Plains had ended, and that its modern history had begun.

The invention of barbed wire was welcomed by farmers and sheep ranchers who did not want their lands overrun by freely-grazing cattle. Many ranchers were so angry to see the range fenced in that shootings occurred between the two groups. The poster for barbed wire (above) was printed in 1880. The sheep are grazing on the Fort Niobrara National Wildlife Refuge in Nebraska.

After the longhorns were rounded up each fall in Texas (above), cowboys drove the cattle north to Kansas cow-towns, such as Dodge City and Abilene. There the cattle were shipped by rail to the East.

A photograph of Dodge City, Kansas, in the 1880's, when it was a wide-open, rip-roaring town, with saloons lining its muddy main street. On the long trail drive, cowhands might have had to fight off Comanches or cattle rustlers. But once they rode into Dodge, cowboys began shooting, fighting, and gambling for pure enjoyment.

As farmers came to the Plains, their plows broke soil which had never been tilled before. They found that the thick prairie sod, tightly woven with grass roots, made fine walls. Sod houses, like this one shown at right, were cool in summer, warm in winter. They grew to be familiar sights on the broad western Plains.

MEN AND MYTHS

Wounded Knee was the burial place of a way of life which had vanished from the West forever.

The Plains Indians' days of greatness, when they followed the buffalo on horseback, had lasted a comparatively short time. But seldom has a primitive people left so distinct a mark on history, or made so deep an impression on the minds of men. Few people today think of the American Indian without imagining the hard-riding, hard-fighting Plains Indian. And although American Indians lived in many different ways, the Plains Indian has come to represent them all.

Even so, he has since been pictured in such an exaggerated way that it is difficult to learn what he was really like.

The story of the life he led, before the coming of the white man, is seldom told. His feelings about making war, and especially about the counting of coups, are hardly ever mentioned. His conflict with the white man is almost never explained from the viewpoint of the Indian.

A few generations ago, all cigar stores had a wooden Indian at the street door.

142

In 1895, George Bird Grinnell, who lived among the Indians and knew them well, said: "We are too apt to forget, that these people are human like ourselves; that they are fathers and mothers, husbands and wives, brothers and sisters; men and women with emotions and passions like our own, even though these feelings are not well regulated and directed in the calm, smoothly flowing channels of civilized life. Not until we recognize this common humanity may we attain the broader view and the wider sympathy which shall give us a true comprehension of the character of the Indian."

But still, many people find it difficult to think of the Indian as a human being. Oliver La Farge, an outstanding authority on the American Indian, traces the white man's false ideas about the red man back to the day when the two first met. In a brilliant essay—*Myths That Hide the American Indian*—La Farge tells how the whites have misunderstood the Indians in a number of ways. First, he said, there was the myth of "the Noble Red Man or the Child of Nature," who either makes long, flowery speeches, or who keeps stupidly silent except for grunting an occasional "Ugh!"

Later, this myth was replaced by another myth, which pictured the

Although these statues were brightly painted, they are now faded with age.

143

Indian as a "ruthless, faithless savage." This, of course, happened during the period after the Civil War when the whites broke treaties to invade Indian territory to gain the gold and land they wanted.

Still later, when the Indian was defeated and forced to live on reservations, the myth changed again. This time, La Farge said, it was useful to make all of the Indians appear to be nothing but "drunken, lazy good-for-nothings."

Throughout American history, one or another of these myths and sometimes several at one time, have been accepted as truth. James Fenimore Cooper's character, Uncas, in *The Last of the Mohicans*, and Henry Wadsworth Longfellow's *Hiawatha* were presented as wise, noble, and sensitive Indians who loved animals, peace, and democracy. The strong, noble profile of the Indian on the old U.S. five cent piece is part of the same myth.

Even the Plains Indian was at first looked upon as a noble red man. But after the Indian fighting which followed the Civil War—the scalping, the torture, the terrifying war cries, Custer's Last Stand, and the Ghost Dance—the white man thought of the Plains Indian only as a cold-blooded savage.

The Wild West shows which toured the East Coast and Europe during the 1890's helped to make this myth popular. Thousands of people flocked to see what were supposed to be actual scenes of Indian warfare. The sight of scores of mounted Indians—sometimes including Sitting Bull—dashing past in mock attacks, made spectators

These palefaced "Indians" starred in The Iron Horse—*a movie made in 1924.*

This cartoon shows the Noble Savage (left) who drinks nothing but pure spring water, and the "drunken good-for-nothing" who has had too much fire water.

think they were getting a glimpse of the real Wild West.

Stirred by Buffalo Bill, who produced one of the best-known Wild West shows, audiences found it easy to imagine blood-thirsty Indians swooping down on innocent men, women, and children. And this mythical Wild West Indian is still kept alive today by books, movies, and television.

Meanwhile, the myth of the lazy, good-for-nothing reservation Indian began to grow popular. This came about during a time when corruption in the Bureau of Indian Affairs had led to wide-scale cheating of the Indians by the whites.

Fortunately, this image of the shiftless Indian has faded. In 1933, the Bureau of Indian Affairs, under the vigorous leadership of John Collier, began an effort to restore dignity to the life of the Indians on the reservations.

Coolidge, while President, was made an honorary Sioux: Chief Leading Eagle.

"Buffalo Bill" Cody's Wild West Show gave its first performance in 1883.

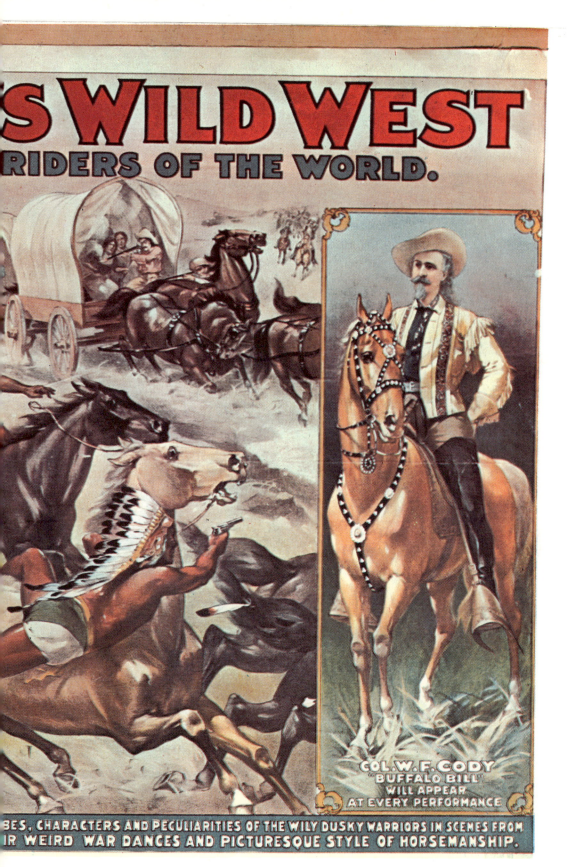

It toured Europe and America, and in 1885 starred Sitting Bull himself.

The Plains Indian and the buffalo were often used on United States coins and bank notes. The famous "buffalo" nickel (above), was struck in 1913.

As a result, the public now thinks of the modern American Indian as a human being who has been badly misunderstood and mistreated in the past and who is now struggling to keep his rightful heritage alive.

For, quite apart from the myths created about him, the real American Indian has real problems to face. He is no longer a "vanishing American." There are more Plains Indians today than there were in 1890, and their number is increasing. And reservation life—which Plains Indians, especially, have always had little use for—continues to be directly opposite to their old free way of life.

But conditions today have improved. Since 1924, all Plains Indians have been citizens of the United States. The Indian Reorganization Act of 1934 gave the Indians the right to establish local governments. to go into business, and to revive Indian ceremonies which had been banned. A form of the Sun Dance is now practiced.

Greater freedom exists on the reservations where Indians dress and live much as do the whites living on nearby farms or ranches. Even so, many of the younger Indians have left the reservations, and moved to the city. This trend was speeded up by World Wars I and II, when Indians once more proved themselves to be first-rate fighting men—a fact which would not have surprised any of the Indian fighters of the nineteenth century.

As more and more Indians make a place for themselves in the modern world—most of today's Indians speak English; many are high school and college graduates—they will realize how much their ancestors have given America.

Numerous place names in the west are reminders of the Plains Indians—the states named Dakota; Cheyenne, the capital of Wyoming;

the counties in Kansas and Texas named Comanche, to mention only a few—just as the names of thousands of other cities, towns, rivers, and mountains in the rest of the country recall other Indian tribes.

Many American expressions and customs owe much to the Indians. Most important of all, some of our basic ideas of democracy and self-government stem from the Indian notion of freedom first observed by European explorers in the seventeenth century.

And yet, despite the existence of real Indians in everyday life, and despite the study of the red man by historians, it is most often the myth-

Indian pennies were first minted in 1859.

In 1908, a $2.50 gold piece (right) appeared.

ical Indian who captures the imagination of people everywhere. It is a cruel joke which history has played on him, and perhaps most harshly on the Plains Indian.

In the years to come, our understanding of the Indian will continue to grow. Perhaps in time we will come closer to knowing the Indian as he really was. But, it is almost certain that the myth of the whooping, war-bonneted, hard-riding Indian brave will never vanish from American folklore. For myths have a way of enduring forever.

A beautiful Indian-head $10 gold piece, or "eagle," sculpted by Augustus Saint-Gaudens, was put in circulation in 1907.

This $5 bill carried a portrait of Sioux Chief Onepapa.

The buffalo on the $10 bill was flanked by Lewis and Clark.

ACKNOWLEDGMENTS The editors are deeply grateful to John C. Ewers, Assistant Director of the Museum of History and Technology of the Smithsonian Institution, for giving tirelessly of his knowledge of American Plains Indians and for his guidance and advice on pictorial material and sources. In addition, they wish expressly to thank the following individuals and organizations for their generous assistance, and for their cooperation in furnishing pictorial matter from their collections: Mr. Hugh Townley of Boston University; Dr. Harold McCracken; Museum of the American Indian—Dr. Frederick J. Dockstader; Smithsonian Institution—Mr. R. A. Elder; Thomas Gilcrease Institute of American History & Art—Mr. James T. Forrest; The Stackpole Company, Harrisburg, Penn.—General E. J. Stackpole; Peabody Museum, Harvard University—Mrs. Katherine B. Edsall; American Museum of Natural History—Mr. Philip C. Gifford, Miss Bella Weitzner; Minnesota Historical Society—Miss Bertha L. Heilbron; State Historical Society of Colorado—Mrs. Laura Allyn Ekstrom; The Reverend P. E. Breton of The Missionaires Oblats de Marie Immaculée, Edmonton, Canada; Dr. William Barclay Parsons of Wilton, Conn.

PICTURE CREDITS

The source of each picture used in this book is listed below, by page. When two or more pictures appear on one page, they are separated by semi-colons. The following abbreviations are used:

AMNH—American Museum of Natural History
CRS—C. R. Smith Collection
LC—Library of Congress
KG—Kennedy Galleries
TG—Thomas Gilcrease Institute of American History and Art
HW—HARPER'S WEEKLY
MAI—Museum of the American Indian
MHS—Minnesota Historical Society
NA—National Archives
NYPL—New York Public Library
PM—Peabody Museum, Harvard University (photographs by Barney Burstein)
SHSC—State Historical Society of Colorado
SI—Smithsonian Institution (photographs by Stanley Manzer)
SI-BAE—Smithsonian Institution, Bureau of American Ethnology
ROM—Royal Ontario Museum, Canada
WPM—West Point Museum Collections

Cover: "Buffalo Hunt—1855," John Mix Stanley —KG. **Front end sheet:** "Ceremony of the Scalps," Frederic Remington—courtesy Harold McCracken. **Half title:** "A Skin Lodge of an Assiniboin Chief," Carl Bodmer, *Travels in the Interior of North America*, Maximilian, Prince zu Wied-Neuwid—NYPL. **Title:** "Fac Simile of an Indian Painting," Bodmer—LC. **Contents:** Colt Fire Arms Mfg. Co. 10 "Buffalo Herd on the Move," William J. Hayes—TG. 12 (top) John Groth; (bot.) T. L. Pattison, Topeka, Kan. 13 George Catlin—AMNH. 14 *Historia General* *de las Indias*, Gómara—LC. **15** SI. **16** (top) Denver Museum of Natural History; (bot.) "Folsom Hunters Spearing Bison," André Durenceau for the NATIONAL GEOGRAPHIC MAGAZINE, © National Geographic Society, Washington, D. C. **17** (top & mid.) SI; (bot.) University of New Mexico. **18** (top) *Quadrupeds of North America*, James J. Audubon—NYPL; (bot.) Catlin—SI. **19** (top) Seth Eastman, *Information respecting the history . . . of the Indian tribes of the United States*, Henry Rowe Schoolcraft—LC; (bot.) Eastman, Schoolcraft, *op. cit.*—NYPL. **20** TG. **23** Map drawn expressly for this book by Elmer Smith. **24** TG. **25** *Indians of the Plains*, Robert H. Lowie—AMNH. **26** Alfred Jacob Miller—Knoedler Art Galleries (J. L. Pulsipher). **28** (top) Peter Rindisbacher—WPM; (bot.) *The Buffalo Hunters*, Mari Sandoz—Hastings House Publishers, Inc. **29** John Fleming, *Narrative of the Canadian Red River*, Henry Youle Hind—NYPL. **30** "A Buffalo Pound," Paul Kane—ROM. **31** PM. **32** (top) MAI; (bot.) HW—NYPL. **33** Eastman, Schoolcraft, *op. cit.*—NYPL. **34** Catlin—AMNH. **36** "A Sioux Village," Catlin—AMNH. **37** (top) Rindisbacher—WPM; (bot.) Catlin—SI. **38** (both) PM. **39** Catlin—NYPL. **40** "Encampment of Piekann Indians near Ft. Clark," Bodmer, Maximilian, *op. cit.*—NYPL. **41** Maximilian, *op. cit.*—LC. **42** (top) KG; (bot. left) HW—NYPL; (bot. right) Bodmer, Maximilian, *op. cit.*—AMNH. **43** (top) *West of Alfred Jacob Miller*, Marvin C. Ross, © 1951 University of Oklahoma Press—Walters Art Gallery; (bot.) KG. **44 & 45** *Pictographs* and *Sign Language of the North American Indians*, Garrick Mallery. **46** (top) KG; (bot.) ROM. **47** (top) SI; (mid. & bot.) Eastman, Schoolcraft, *op. cit.*—NYPL. **48** (top) Bodmer, Maximilian, *op. cit.*—NYPL; (bot.) Catlin—NYPL. **49** (top) Maximilian, *op. cit.*—LC; (bot. left) HW—NYPL; (bot. right) Bodmer, Maximilian, *op. cit.*—AMNH. **50** (top & mid.) MAI; (bot.) SI. **51** (top) SI; (mid.) MAI; (bot. left) AMNH; (bot. right) SI. **52** (top) SI; (mid.) Bodmer, Maximilian, *op. cit.*—NYPL; (bot.) Bodmer, Maximilian, *op. cit.*—AMNH. **53** (top) SI; (mid.) HARPER'S MONTHLY—NYPL; (bot. left) Remington, *Song of Hiawatha*, Henry Wadsworth Longfellow—NYPL; (bot. right) Stanley, Schoolcraft, *op. cit.*—NYPL. **54** City Art Museum, St. Louis. **56** (top) "Indian Taking Scalp," Rindisbacher—WPM; (bot.) SI. **57** (top) Catlin, *Illustrations of the Manners . . . of the North American Indians*—NYPL; (bot.) Eastman, Schoolcraft, *op. cit.*—NYPL. **58** (top) Catlin—KG; (bot.) Maximilian, *op. cit.*—NYPL. **59** Catlin—AMNH. **61** Catlin—KG. **62** SI. **63** (top) Eastman, Schoolcraft, *op. cit.*—NYPL; (bot.) SI. **64** Catlin—AMNH. **66** Eastman, Schoolcraft, *op. cit.*—NYPL. **67** (both) Lowie, *op. cit.*—AMNH. **68** ROM. **69** Catlin—SI. **70** "Offering of the Mandan Indians," Bodmer, Maximilian, *op. cit.*—NYPL. **71** (both) MAI. **72** TG. **74** Map drawn expressly for this book by Elmer Smith. **74 & 75** *A Journal of the Travels of . . . Capt. Lewis and Capt. Clark 1812*, Patrick Gass—NYPL. **76** "The Weak Never Started," Boundy, after Wimar—CRS. **78** *Rocky Mountain Saints*, Thomas B. M. Stenhouse—NYPL. **79** HW—NYPL. **80** (top left) *Buffalo Land*, W. E. Webb—NYPL; (top right) Henry H. Cross—TG; (mid.) Missouri State Hist. Soc.; (bot.) George Caleb Bingham—Detroit Institute of Arts. **81** (top) "The Moun-

tain Man," Oscar Berninghaus—CRS; (bot.) HW—NYPL. **82** (top) NYPL; (bot.) *River of the West*, Frances F. Victor—Oregon Hist. Soc. **83** (top & bot.) *Life, Letters, Travels*, Pierre Jean de Smet—NYPL; Picture Chart—L'Institut de Missiologie—University of Ottawa. **84** LC. **85** de Smet, *op. cit.*—NYPL. **86** Miller—TG. **87** Miller, Ross, *op. cit.*, © 1951 University of Oklahoma Press—Walters Art Gallery. **88** (top) HW—NYPL; (bot.) Cross—TG. **89** SI-BAE. **90** (top) *Commerce of the Pirates*, Josiah Gregg—NYPL; (bot.) Maximilian, *op. cit.*—Mariners' Museum. **91** (top) "Ships of the Plains," Samuel Colman—Union League Club of New York; (bot.) Eastman, Schoolcraft, *op. cit.*—NYPL. **92** (top) Maximilian, *op. cit.*—NYPL; (bot.) Frederic Remington, Harold McCracken—courtesy J. B. Lippincott Co. **93** (both) HUTCHINGS CALIFORNIA MAGAZINE—Bancroft Library. **94** "On the Warpath"—MHS. **96** Anton Gag—MHS. **97** (top) James McGrew—MHS; (bot.) James Fairman—Sibley County Hist. Soc. **98** (top) Cross—TG; (bot.) T. W. Wood—MHS. **99** Stevens—MHS. **100** SHSC. **101** Map drawn expressly for this book by Elmer Smith. **103** Robert Lindneux—SHSC. **104** Map from *Indian Fights & Fighters*, Cyrus T. Brady—NYPL. **106** (top) Olaf C. Seltzer—TG; (bot.) SI-BAE. **107** Cross—TG. **108** (top) NA; (bot.) SHSC. **109** (left & cen.) NA; (right) SHSC. **110** (top) HW—NYPL; (bot.) Cross—TG. **111** (top) Collection of William Barclay Parsons; (bot.) Union Pacific Railroad. **112** (top right) LC; (top left) Yale University Library; (bot.) HW—NYPL. **113** (top) HW—NYPL; (bot.) MHS. **114** Cross—TG. **115** "Thornburgh's Battlefield; White River Massacre," Frank Tenney Johnson—CRS. **116** (top l. to r.) TG; LC; TG; NA; (bot.) HW—NYPL. **117** HW—NYPL. **118** (both) Cross—TG. **119** Charles Schreyvogel—TG. **120** (both) SI-BAE. **122 & 123** (all) Cross—TG. **124** Northern Pacific Railroad. **125** Reno, Cross—TG; (bot.) Seltzer—TG. **126** W. R. Leigh—The Woolaroc Museum. **128** (top) SI; (bot.) Stanley Vestal. **129** (top) HW—NYPL; (mid.) Collections of John S. du Mont; (bot.) Stanley Vestal. **130** "Custer's Last Fight," Gayle Hoskins, *The Custer Myth*, Col. W. A. Graham—The Stackpole Co., Harrisburg, Penna. **132** SI-BAE. **133** NYPL. **134** Mary I. Wright. *Ghost Dance Religion*, James A. Mooney—SI-BAE. **135** HW—NYPL. **136** (top) Mooney, *op. cit.*—SI-BAE; (bot.) *Calendar History of the Kiowa Indians*, Mooney—SI-BAE. **137** *Ghost Dance Religion*, Mooney—SI-BAE; (bot.) MAI. **138** (top) Cross—TG; (mid.) NA. **139** Seltzer—TG. **140** (top) U. S. Steel; (bot.) U. S. Dept. Agriculture. **141** (top) LC; (mid.) Kansas State Hist. Soc.; (bot.) Nebraska State Hist. Soc. **142 & 143** Collection of Helena Penrose. **144** (top) LESLIE'S ILLUSTRATED WEEKLY—NYPL; (bot.) Museum of Modern Art, Film Library. **145** (top) Webb, *op. cit.*—NYPL; (bot.) World Wide Photos. **146** LC. **148 & 149** Paper money & $10 gold piece—courtesy of Gimbel's Coin Dept., N. Y. C.; other coins—American Numismatic Soc. **Index:** "Warrior Sacrificing His Horse," Catlin—KG. **Back end sheet:** "Medicine Pipe-Stem Dance," Paul Kane—ROM. **Back Cover:** *Riding in the Hot P.M. with Umbrella*—Milwaukee County Historical Society, photograph courtesy of Hugh Townley.

BIBLIOGRAPHY

Bolton, Herbert E. *Coronado, Knight of Pueblo and Plains*. Albuquerque, N. M.: University of New Mexico Press, 1949.

Brebner, John B. *The Explorers of North America*. New York: Doubleday, 1955.

Catlin, George. *Letters and Notes on the Manners, Customs and Condition of the North American Indians*. New York: Wiley & Putnam, 1841.

Collier, John. *The Indians of the Americas*. New York: W. W. Norton, 1947.

De Voto, Bernard A. *Across the Wide Missouri*. Boston: Houghton Mifflin Co., 1947.

De Voto, Bernard A. *The Course of Empire*. Boston: Houghton Mifflin Co., 1952.

Dodge, Richard I. *Our Wild Indians*. Hartford: Worthington & Co., 1882.

Downey, Fairfax. *Indian Fighting Army*. New York: Scribner's, 1941.

Ewers, John C. *The Blackfeet: Raiders on the Northwestern Plains*. Norman, Okla.: University of Oklahoma Press, 1958.

Grinnell, George B. *The Cheyenne Indians*. New Haven: Yale Univ. Press, 1923.

Grinnell, George B. *The Fighting Cheyennes*. Oklahoma Press, 1956.

Grinnell, George B. *The Story of the Indian*. New York: Appleton, 1923.

Hamilton, Charles. *Cry of the Tunderbird*. New York: Macmillan Co., 1950.

Hodge, Frederick W. (ed.). *Handbook of American Indians North of Mexico*. Washington, D. C.: Bureau of American Ethnology, Smithsonian Institution, 1907–1910.

Hyde, George E. *Red Cloud's Folk: A History of the Oglala Sioux Indians*. Oklahoma Press, 1937.

Hyde, George E. *A Sioux Chronicle*. Oklahoma Press, 1956.

Johnson, Vance. *Heaven's Tableland*. New York: Farrar Straus, 1947.

Kraenzel, Carl Frederick. *The Great Plains in Transition*. Oklahoma Press, 1955.

La Farge, Oliver. (ed.). *The Changing Indian*. Oklahoma Press, 1942.

Llewellyn, Karl N., and Hoebel, E. Adamson. *The Cheyenne Way*. Norman: University of Oklahoma Press, 1941.

Lowie, Robert H. *Indians of the Plains*. New York: McGraw-Hill, 1954.

Mooney, James. *The Ghost Dance Religion and the Sioux Outbreak of 1890*. Washington, D. C.: Bureau of American Ethnology, Smithsonian Institution, 1896.

Roe, Frank G. *The Indian and the Horse*. Oklahoma Press, 1955.

Sandoz, Mari. *The Buffalo Hunters*. New York: Hastings House, 1954.

Sandoz, Mari. *The Cattlemen*. New York: Hastings House, 1958.

Sandoz, Mari. *Cheyenne Autumn*. New York: McGraw-Hill, 1953.

Sandoz, Mari. *Crazy Horse, the Strange Man of the Oglalas*. New York: Knopf, 1942.

Schmitt, Martin F., and Brown, Dee. *Fighting Indians of the West*. New York: Charles Scribner's Sons, 1955.

Stewart, Edgar I. *Custer's Luck*. Norman: University of Oklahoma Press, 1955.

Underhill, Ruth M. *Red Man's America*. Chicago: Univ. of Chicago Press, 1953.

Vestal, Stanley. *New Sources of Indian History*. Oklahoma Press, 1934.

Vestal, Stanley. *Sitting Bull, Champion of the Sioux*. Boston: Houghton Mifflin Co., 1957.

Vestal, Stanley. *Warpath*. Boston: Houghton Mifflin Co., 1934.

Vestal, Stanley. *Warpath and Council Fire*. New York: Random House, 1948.

Wallace, Ernest, and Hoebel, E. Adamson. *The Comanches, Lords of the South Plains*. Oklahoma Press, 1952.

Webb, Walter Prescott. *The Great Plains*. Boston: Ginn & Co., 1931.

Wellman, Paul I. *Death on the Prairie, the Thirty Years Struggle for the Western Plains*. New York: Macmillan Co., 1934.

Wissler, Clark. *The American Indian*. New York: Oxford University Press, 1922.

Wissler, Clark. *Indians of the United States*. New York: Doubleday & Co., 1940.

FOR FURTHER READING

Young readers seeking further information on Indians of the Plains will find the following books to be both helpful and entertaining:

Downey, Fairfax. *Indian Fighting Army*. New York: Scribner's, 1941.

Ewers, John C. *The Blackfeet: Raiders on the Northwestern Plains*. Norman: University of Oklahoma Press, 1958.

Garst, Shannon. *Crazy Horse, Great Warrior of the Sioux*. Boston: Houghton Mifflin Co. 1950.

Grinnell, George B. *The Fighting Cheyennes*. Oklahoma Press, 1956.

Hyde, George E. *Red Cloud's Folk: A History of the Oglala Sioux Indians*. Oklahoma Press, 1937.

Lowie, Robert H. *Indians of the Plains*. New York: McGraw-Hill, 1954.

Marriott, Alice. *Indians on Horseback*. New York: Thomas Y. Crowell Co., 1948.

Marriott, Alice. *Winter-Telling Stories*. New York: Wm. Sloane Assoc. Inc., 1947.

Parkman, Francis. *The Oregon Trail*. New York: Doubleday & Co., 1959.

Standing Bear, Luther. *My People the Sioux*. Boston: Houghton Mifflin, 1928.

Sandoz, Mari. *Crazy Horse, the Strange Man of the Oglalas*. New York: Knopf, 1942.

Schmitt, Martin F., and Brown, Dee. *Fighting Indians of the West*. New York: Charles Scribner's Sons, 1955.

Vestal, Stanley. *Sitting Bull, Champion of the Sioux*. Oklahoma Press, 1957.

Wallace, Ernest, and Hoebel, E. Adamson. *The Comanches, Lords of the South Plains*. Oklahoma Press, 1952.

Wellman, Paul I. *Death on the Prairie, the Thirty Years Struggle for the Western Plains*. New York: Macmillan Co., 1934.

Wissler, Clark. *Indians of the United States*. New York: Doubleday & Co., 1940.

INDEX

Bold face indicates pages on which illustrations appear.

AMERICAN HERITAGE PUBLISHING CO., INC. • BOOK DIVISION: Richard M. Ketchum, *Editor.*
JUNIOR LIBRARY: Ferdinand N. Monjo, *Editor,* John Ratti, *Assistant Editor.* Malabar Schleiter •
Judy Sheftel • Julia B. Potts • Mary Leverty, *Editorial Assistants. Designed by Jos. Trautwein.*